Contents

"The important thing is not to stop questioning. Curiosity has its own reason for existence."

— Albert Einstein

1. Exploring the Quantum Frontier

In an era marked by technological wonder and exploration, the boundaries of what once seemed impossible are steadily being redrawn. One of the fascinating frontiers that scientists now approach with careful steps is the enigmatic field of quantum mechanics. In the midst of particle chess and wave functions, a particularly intriguing concept emerges—a potential application that not only captures the imagination but also promises to redefine our daily interactions with reality: Quantum Proxy, the feasibility of telepresence through quantum entanglement.

Imagine being able to instantly project yourself into another location, sharing experiences as if you were physically there. The magic lies in the delicate dance of particles, entwined beyond our traditional comprehension of speed and distance. It evokes the notion of living on the seamless edge of presence, where physics meets technology in a mind-bending alliance.

This book begins by demystifying the fundamental principles, obligations, and thrilling possibilities behind quantum mechanics and entanglement, with a straightforward approach designed to guide you through each groundbreaking chapter. We prepare to delve into the cutting-edge science and ethical considerations as we explore how this transformative technology can reshape everything from communication to our very sense of connection in the world. Join us in unraveling the fabric of space and time—welcome to the exploration of Quantum Proxy.

2. Foundation of Quantum Mechanics

2.1. The Birth of Quantum Theory

The journey toward the birth of quantum theory is as intricate and captivating as the science it introduced. The roots of this revolutionary field trace back to the late 19th and early 20th centuries, a period intertwined with the advancement of classical physics. This era saw unprecedented strides in our understanding of the physical universe, but it also presented challenges that traditional physics struggled to address, ultimately leading to the formulation of quantum mechanics.

One significant frontier was the behavior of light. During this time, light was largely understood through the perspective of wave theory, primarily due to the works of scientists like James Clerk Maxwell. He had brilliantly theorized that light was an electromagnetic wave, a revolutionary concept that explained a multitude of optical phenomena. However, experiments in the late 19th century, including the photoelectric effect, began to highlight peculiarities that could not be reconciled with classical physics. In particular, when light of certain frequencies struck a metal surface, it led to the ejection of electrons, and the behavior of these electrons suggested that light exhibited characteristics of particles—a paradox that laid the groundwork for a quantum shift in our understanding.

Max Planck is often heralded as the father of quantum theory. In 1900, he introduced the idea that energy could be emitted or absorbed only in discrete units or "quanta." This notion emerged from his work on blackbody radiation, which sought to understand how objects emitted thermal radiation. Traditional theories predicted that energy emission should increase indefinitely with frequency, leading to predictions dubbed the "ultraviolet catastrophe." Planck proposed instead that energy thresholds existed for different frequencies, thus introducing the concept of quantization in energy levels. His revolutionary equation, $E=hf$ (where E is energy, h is Planck's constant, and f is frequency), encapsulated this idea that energy is proportional to frequency, paving the way for the then-radical acceptance of quantum mechanics.

Around the same time, Albert Einstein expanded on Planck's concept through his explanation of the photoelectric effect in 1905. Einstein proposed that light itself was composed of particles, which he termed "photons." This idea reconciled the wave-particle duality of light, suggesting that photons could exhibit properties of both waves and particles. His insights caused a stir, leading physicists to reconsider the nature of light and matter fundamentally. Einstein's work not only won him the Nobel Prize in Physics in 1921 but also laid the ground-work for future exploration into quantum phenomena, capturing the essence of the burgeoning field of quantum theory.

As the initial seeds of quantum theory sprouted, another pivotal idea emerged: the principle of wave-particle duality. This principle suggested that not only could light exhibit both wave-like and parti-cle-like behavior, but so too could matter. The De Broglie hypothesis introduced the revolutionary notion that particles, such as electrons, could also have wave-like characteristics, leading to the concept that all matter exhibits both waves and particles depending on the circum-stances of observation. This idea culminated in the formulation of what would become the wave function, an essential component of quantum mechanics that describes the probability distribution of a particle's position or momentum.

This concept was further solidified through the pioneering work of Niels Bohr and his atomic model in 1913. Bohr introduced quantized orbits for electrons in atoms, suggesting that electrons could only oc-cupy specific energy levels. While Bohr's model elegantly explained phenomena such as the hydrogen spectrum, it was still anchored in classical ideas, leading to further challenges that required deeper exploration into the nature of reality at the quantum level.

As the fabric of quantum theory continued to unfold, it became evident that particles do not exist in definite states until they are observed. This was encapsulated in the Copenhagen interpretation, primarily formulated by Niels Bohr and Werner Heisenberg in the 1920s. The principle of superposition was introduced, positing that particles could exist in multiple states or locations simultaneously until a measurement collapses them into a singular state. This facet of quantum theory challenged the classical deterministic view of the universe, introducing concepts of probabilities and uncertainty, encapsulated in Heisenberg's Uncertainty Principle.

In essence, the birth of quantum theory reshaped the landscape of physics by challenging conventional understandings of reality. The implications of these early discoveries propelled scientists into new realms of inquiry, leading to the development of sophisticated theories that would give rise to revolutionary technologies, including semiconductors, lasers, and, eventually, quantum computing.

This historical tapestry illustrates how the birth of quantum theory was not merely a collection of breakthroughs but an evolution of thought that redefined our understanding of the universe. The advent of quantum theory set in motion a cascade of scientific advancements that blurred the lines between physics, philosophy, and technology, transforming our comprehension of existence itself, and laying a crucial foundation for the discussions and applications we explore in the realm of Quantum Proxy and telepresence through quantum entanglement. As we navigate this new era, the echoes of quantum theory's birth remind us that within the enigmatic dance of particles lies the ultimate potential to redefine our connection with reality.

2.2. Understanding Light and Particle Duality

The exploration of light and particle duality stands at the very heart of modern quantum mechanics, presenting a paradigm that redefines our understanding of nature. This concept underlies the myriad phenomena observed in the quantum realm, urging us to reconsider not only how we perceive light but also the fundamental building blocks of reality itself.

Historically, the nature of light has been a topic of avid debate. In classical physics, light was predominantly characterized as a wave, a convention solidified by the pioneering work of scientists like Thomas Young, whose double-slit experiment demonstrated interference patterns akin to those produced by water waves. This wave theory coherently explained various optical phenomena, such as diffraction and polarization. However, as the 19th century progressed, experimental findings began to challenge this predominant wave theory, particularly with phenomena such as the photoelectric effect.

The photoelectric effect, described prominently by Albert Einstein, showcased how light could induce the emission of electrons from a metal surface. What was perplexing was that this effect appeared to depend solely on the light's frequency and not on its intensity, illuminating the fact that light also exhibited particle-like behavior. The notion of light as quantized packets of energy, or photons, hinged on the assertion that it could act as both a wave and a particle, embodying the essence of duality.

This wave-particle duality is not a mere oddity of light but extends to all matter, a revelation crystallized by the groundbreaking hypothesis of Louis de Broglie. In 1924, de Broglie proposed that particles, much like light, exhibit wave characteristics. This revolutionary idea suggested a fundamental interconnectedness between waves and particles at the quantum level, fundamentally challenging the classical notions that confined particles to discrete points in space and time.

Wave-particle duality is more than an abstract characterization; it is fundamentally tied to the principles and mathematical frameworks that define quantum mechanics. The wave function, a cornerstone of this framework, encapsulates all information about a quantum system, representing probabilities of finding a particle in various states or locations. In essence, before measurement, a particle exists in a superposition of states, where it can behave both like a wave and like a particle, but this duality collapses to a single outcome upon observation.

The implications of wave-particle duality resonate throughout modern physics, revealing a deeper level of reality where certainty unravels into probabilities. This realization ushered in a new era of scientific thought, challenging classical determinism and the very concept of reality. The uncertainties and probabilistic outcomes highlight a reality that is interlaced with complexities and paradoxes, compelling scientists and philosophers alike to grapple with the implications of what it means to observe and measure.

As we seek to derive tangible applications from quantum mechanics, such as those anticipated in Quantum Proxy, understanding light and particle duality becomes paramount. The potential for utilizing entangled states, where two particles influence each other irrespective of distance, hinges on acknowledging and manipulating the dual nature of particles. The concept challenges the linear perception of communication and interaction, enabling instant connectivity that defies classical limitations of space and time.

In the realm of Quantum Proxy, the expectations merge technological innovation with the enriched understanding of quantum fundamentals. If we can harness wave-particle duality effectively, we stand on the precipice of redefining telepresence. Such technology wouldn't merely allow for remote communication but would instead bridge distances as if they were nonexistent, responding to the intrinsic nature of reality where the classical boundaries dissolve.

Moreover, as we integrate this knowledge into practical applications, the ethical and philosophical dimensions surfacing from the quantum domain beckon scrutiny. If we inhabit a world illuminated by such dualities, how do we define presence, identity, and interaction? Our journey through quantum mechanics, punctuated by light and particle duality, serves as the foundation for exploring not just groundbreaking technological advancements but also the very essence of human connection in an evolving reality.

In summary, the understanding of light and particle duality is both a tribute to the intricacies of quantum phenomena and a guiding principle as we venture into the future of communication technologies. It is an invitation to reconcile the complexities and mysteries of the quantum world, and it holds the key to unlocking transformative experiences that lie in the nascent potential of Quantum Proxy. As we chart our path forward, the dual nature of light and matter will illuminate each step, guiding our exploration of connections that extend beyond conventional boundaries.

2.3. The Emergence of Quantum State

The emergence of the quantum state represents a pivotal evolution in the understanding of the quantum realm, providing the foundational basis for much of modern quantum mechanics. Unlike classical states, where objects can be precisely defined by their position and velocity at any given moment, quantum states introduce a level of complexity characterized by uncertainty and the probabilistic nature of existence. This subchapter delves into the intricacies of quantum states, their behaviors, and their implications as we navigate the concepts pivotal to the notion of Quantum Proxy.

At the core of quantum mechanics lies the idea that particles exist not in fixed states but within a vast landscape of possibilities. When we discuss a quantum state, we refer to the set of information that describes a system's properties at the quantum level. The formal representation of this information is encapsulated in the mathematical object known as the wave function, denoted typically by the Greek letter psi (Ψ). This wave function contains all the probabilistic information about a quantum system, being a critical tool for connecting theoretical predictions with empirical outcomes.

The wave function signifies a departure from classical determinism. In classical physics, a particle is considered to possess definite properties, such as location and momentum, at all times. In contrast, in quantum mechanics, the wave function encapsulates the idea that a particle can concurrently inhabit multiple states. This phenomenon is known as superposition, where a particle exists in a combination of all possible states until it is measured. An apt demonstration of this principle is exemplified in Schrödinger's famous thought experiment involving a cat in a box, where the cat is neither alive nor dead until observed, illustrating the uncanny nature of superposition and measurement in quantum mechanics.

The collapse of the wave function—a critical aspect of the measurement process—further solidifies the role of observation in defining a quantum state. When a measurement is made, the probabilities assigned to various outcomes effectively "collapse" the wave function, resulting in the manifestation of a observable state from the realm of possibilities. This act of measurement becomes essential, as it is this interaction that ultimately manifests reality as we perceive it. The implications of this behavior are profound, as they challenge conventional notions of reality and prompt new philosophical questions surrounding existence and knowledge.

Additionally, quantum states can exhibit entanglement—a phenomenon where the properties of multiple particles become interconnected, regardless of the distance separating them. When entangled, the measurement of one particle instantaneously influences the state of another particle, a property that defies classical understandings of causality and locality. This interdependence persists even when particles are separated by vast distances, leading to the description of entanglement as "spooky action at a distance," famously coined by Einstein. The emergence of entangled quantum states opens the door to applications that venture beyond mere theoretical speculation, providing fertile ground for exploring technologies such as Quantum Proxy.

Understanding quantum states is integral to developing the principles that underpin Quantum Proxy technology. The notion of telepresence through quantum entanglement hinges on the ability to manipulate and exploit these quantum states. If we can harness entangled particles to serve as proxies for distant locations, it would redefine interactions, creating pathways for instantaneous communication and experiential sharing that transcend the traditional limits of distance and time.

In practical terms, researchers are actively investigating how quantum states can be manipulated and engineered to facilitate unique applications in various fields. The pursuit of quantum computing, for example, relies on the coherence and control of quantum states to perform calculations at speeds impossible for classical computers. Quantum bits, or qubits, operate in superpositions of states, leading to the potential for solving complex problems with unprecedented efficiency. Moreover, the realization of quantum networks for enhanced communication systems is one of the burgeoning areas of interest, where quantum states enable secure information transfer impervious to interception.

Beyond their practical applications, quantum states also invite ethical and philosophical considerations. The realization that measurements can alter the state of systems challenges our understanding of observer effects and has implications for privacy and consent in technologies that utilize quantum entanglement. How do we define the nature and scope of presence or identity when atomic interactions can span temporal and spatial dimensions? As we embrace the possibilities offered by Quantum Proxy, it becomes essential to ponder these implications, stimulating discourse on the responsibilities accompanying such profound capabilities.

As we venture deeper into the implications of quantum states within the broader context of Quantum Proxy, it is evident that these states are more than abstract mathematical constructs. They encapsulate the essence of a new reality that transcends our conventional understanding of space and time, laying the groundwork for technological innovations that could reshape human interaction and connectivity on a global scale. The quantum state emerges not just as a scientific concept, but as a gateway into a future where the boundaries of presence dissolve, forging pathways into realms of experience previously confined to the imagination. The legacy of quantum states, intertwined with entanglement and superposition, will illuminate our quest for deeper connections in an ever-evolving technological landscape.

2.4. Core Principles and Postulates

The core principles and postulates of quantum mechanics serve as the bedrock upon which the vast and intricate edifice of quantum theory is built. These principles not only guide scientific exploration but also redefine our perceptions of reality itself. Understanding these principles is essential as we delve into the realm of Quantum Proxy, where the application of quantum entanglement holds the potential to revolutionize concepts of presence and connection.

At the heart of quantum theory is the principle of superposition, which posits that a quantum system can exist simultaneously in multiple states until it is measured. This defies classical mechanics, where objects have definite positions and velocities. Instead, in quantum mechanics, particles such as electrons are described by wave functions that encapsulate various probabilities for their attributes. This principle invites both wonder and challenge, prompting critical examination of what reality is when it is not being observed. It leads us to question the foundational beliefs about existence and causality. Superposition lays the groundwork for phenomena such as quantum entanglement, where particles become intertwined in such a way that the state of one instantly influences the other, no matter the distance separating them.

The next principle is the concept of entanglement itself. This phenomenon occurs when two or more quantum particles become connected in such a way that the state of one particle cannot be described independently of the state of another, even when separated by vast distances. The implications of entanglement render traditional views of separateness and independence profoundly inadequate. Here, the universe unveils a tapestry of interconnectedness, fundamentally challenging the classical understanding of locality. This realization enriches the dialogue surrounding Quantum Proxy and informs our approach to developing technologies that exploit such non-local phenomena.

The uncertainty principle, articulated by Werner Heisenberg, further complicates classical interpretations. It states that certain pairs of physical properties, like position and momentum, cannot both be precisely measured at the same time. The more accurately we measure one, the less accurately we can measure the other. This fundamental limitation emphasizes that at the quantum level, reality is not fixed; instead, it embodies an intrinsic unpredictability. The uncertainty principle highlights the inherent limitations of our knowledge and challenges our conceptualization of determinism.

Complementing these principles are the postulates governing quantum mechanics. One foundational postulate is that the state of a quantum system is completely described by its wave function, which evolves according to the Schrödinger equation. This postulate forms the basis for predicting the behavior of quantum systems and reinforces the idea that we are not merely observers but active participants in the unfolding of quantum reality.

Another pivotal postulate is the relationship between measurement and probability. When a measurement is made, the wave function collapses, leading to a definitive outcome from a range of possibilities. This postulate introduces the act of observation as a critical component of reality itself, suggesting that our interactions with quantum systems directly shape the fabric of existence. In the context of Quantum Proxy, understanding how measurements influence particle states and the coalescence of possibilities into singular outcomes becomes crucial for successfully harnessing telepresence technologies.

Finally, an essential postulate relates to the exchange of information. Quantum mechanics posits that information itself possesses a fundamental role in the universe, dictated by the laws of quantum mechanics. The transfer of information through quantum states, especially in entangled systems, establishes protocols for secure communication that classical methods cannot replicate. Quantum key distribution, for instance, leverages these principles to create communication channels that remain secure against eavesdropping.

Through the lens of these core principles and postulates, we can appreciate the intricacies and marvels of the quantum realm. They underscore the fundamental interconnectedness of quantum systems, uniting disparate phenomena into a cohesive narrative that encompasses everything from the microscopic behavior of particles to the macro-level implications for technology and society.

As we forge ahead in applying these principles to the development of Quantum Proxy technology, we are not merely innovating; we are engaging with an evolving relationship between physics and consciousness. The ability to connect distant realities and share experiences through quantum entanglement unravels traditional notions of presence and closeness. Navigating this rich landscape demands that we remain mindful of the implications and responsibilities that arise from harnessing such transformative technologies.

The exploration of these core principles and postulates serves as a compass guiding us through uncharted territories. It calls on us to grapple with both the potential and the limitations of our scientific endeavors, acknowledging that as we venture deeper into quantum mechanics, we also venture deeper into the essence of what it means to connect, interact, and exist in a universe that continually defies our expectations. The insights gleaned from understanding these fundamentals will illuminate the path toward realizing the ambitions of Quantum Proxy, bridging distances, and propelling us toward a future where the boundaries of human experience are redefined.

2.5. Entanglement and Non-locality

The concept of quantum entanglement unveils a fascinating layer of our understanding of the quantum universe, leading us to confront notions of space, time, and locality that have been foundational to classical physics. At its core, entanglement describes a phenomenon where pairs or groups of quantum particles become interconnected such that the state of one particle cannot be described independently of the state of another, even when the particles are separated by vast distances. This remarkably non-local characteristic challenges traditional ideas of separability and locality, which have governed physics since Newton's time.

To fully appreciate the implications of entanglement, it is vital to delve into its historical background and the foundational experiments that illuminated this enigmatic phenomenon. The roots of quantum entanglement can be traced back to the early 20th century when the groundwork for quantum theory was being established. Notable physicists, including Albert Einstein, Niels Bohr, and Erwin Schrödinger, played crucial roles in shaping the initial discussions around quantum mechanics and its peculiarities.

Einstein, who was initially skeptical about the completeness of quantum mechanics, famously critiqued the idea of entanglement with his phrase "spooky action at a distance." He posited that quantum mechanics could not reconcile with the principles of locality that were integral to classical physics. In 1935, in collaboration with Podolsky and Rosen, he introduced the Einstein-Podolsky-Rosen (EPR) paradox, a thought experiment designed to highlight what he perceived as the inadequacies of quantum mechanics. The EPR paradox posed the scenario of two entangled particles, suggesting that measuring one particle instantaneously determined the state of the other, regardless of the distance separating them. Einstein argued that this instantaneous communication violated the principles of relativity, which maintains that information cannot travel faster than the speed of light.

Awareness of entanglement's implications took decades to develop, with significant advancements in experimental techniques eventually lending support to the phenomenon. Subsequent experiments, notably those conducted by physicist Alain Aspect in the 1980s, sought to test the predictions made by quantum mechanics against the principles of locality. Aspect's experiments provided compelling evidence that entangled particles correlate their behaviors instantaneously, thereby reinforcing the validity of quantum mechanics and entanglement while raising provocative questions about the nature of reality itself.

Mathematically, entanglement can be described using the framework of quantum mechanics, particularly through the formalism of wave functions and tensor products. The simplest representation of entangled states can be observed in the case of two qubits, which can exist in a superposition of states described by a Bell state, such as $(|00\rangle + |11\rangle)/\sqrt{2}$. When such qubits are measured, the outcome is correlated: if one qubit is measured to be $|0\rangle$, the other must also be $|0\rangle$, and similarly for the state $|1\rangle$. This stark contrast to classical correlations invites us to rethink our understanding of information and measurement in quantum systems.

Beyond its theoretical underpinnings, entanglement offers a wide array of applications that extend far beyond the classical physics paradigm. It serves as a cornerstone for emerging technologies such as quantum cryptography, which leverages entangled states to ensure secure communication. In principles such as Quantum Key Distribution (QKD), parties can share encryption keys that are proven secure against eavesdropping—a feat rooted in the properties of entangled photons.

Additionally, entanglement is fundamental to the development of quantum computing, where entangled qubits perform complex calculations at an unprecedented pace. Quantum computers operate through manipulating these entangled states, potentially solving problems that are intractable for classical computers. This opens new frontiers in various fields, including cryptography, optimization, and materials science.

The implications of entanglement extend to our understanding of space and time itself. Quantum entanglement suggests that the classical notion of locality—where objects are only directly influenced by their immediate surroundings—may need to be reevaluated. Entangled particles, seemingly in disparate locations, communicate instantaneously, pointing to a deeper, interconnected fabric of reality. This challenges the conventional delineation of space and time, suggesting that information may transcend the limits imposed by the speed of light, thus reshaping our conception of causality and the interrelations within the universe.

As we venture into the conceptual landscape of Quantum Proxy, the knowledge surrounding entanglement and non-locality lays the groundwork for envisioning a new era of communication technology. The potential of telepresence through quantum entanglement holds the promise of bridging distances in real-time, creating experiences that resonate with an individual's consciousness as if they were co-located. This redefinition of presence challenges our preconceptions of interaction, ultimately reshaping how we conceive of connection and reality in an ever-evolving technological landscape.

In summary, entanglement and its non-local characteristics propel us into a realm where the conventional boundaries of reality become fluid and interconnected. Through understanding this enigmatic phenomenon, we not only grapple with the subtleties of quantum mechanics but unlock doors to transformative technologies that hold profound implications for humanity. As we explore the concepts of Quantum Proxy and telepresence, the intricate dance of particles connected beyond space and time will serve as the foundation for our ongoing journey into the future of human interaction.

3. Quantum Entanglement Fundamentals

3.1. Historical Background of Entanglement

The historical background of quantum entanglement unfolds within a tapestry woven from relentless intellectual curiosity and groundbreaking scientific endeavor. This complex narrative intertwines not merely the advances in theoretical frameworks but also the moments of philosophical introspection that shaped our understanding of reality itself. The seeds of entanglement were sown alongside the birth of quantum mechanics in the early 20th century when the established notions of physics were rigorously challenged.

In the early years of quantum theory, significant advancements catalyzed by pioneering figures such as Max Planck, Albert Einstein, and Niels Bohr paved the road for later explorations of entanglement. Quantum mechanics emerged from the quest to explain phenomena that classical physics found inscrutable, providing a new lens through which to view the subatomic world. A crucial aspect of this new perspective was the realization that particles could exist in states of superposition, simultaneously occupying multiple probabilities until measurement crystallized one outcome.

Einstein's seminal work on the photoelectric effect laid significant groundwork for these developments, demonstrating the dual nature of light and propelling the idea that matter, too, could exhibit wave-particle duality. He, along with contemporaries such as Niels Bohr, soon became embroiled in discussions surrounding the implications of quantum theory on determinism and locality. It was within this philosophical battleground that the idea of entanglement began to take shape.

The term "entanglement" itself was popularized by Erwin Schrödinger in 1935 during his critique of the emerging interpretations of quantum mechanics. Schrödinger's vision of entanglement articulated how particles could become interlinked into a cohesive quantum state—an idea that sparked considerable debate about the fundamental nature of reality. Notably, in a thought experiment that would eventually bear his name, Schrödinger posed a scenario involving two particles whose states became instantaneously correlated regardless of the distance separating them. This remarkable relationship transcended classical notions of space and time, leading to what Einstein would later dismiss as "spooky action at a distance."

Schrödinger's perspectives echoed through the scientific community and became the impetus for the Einstein-Podolsky-Rosen (EPR) paradox, developed as a means to argue against the completeness of quantum mechanics. The EPR paper raised significant concerns about the implications of entangled states and the role of measurement in determining reality. Here, Einstein expressed his disbelief in the randomness inherent in quantum mechanics, positing instead that particles should possess definite states independent of observation. He emphasized the seemingly paradoxical nature of entanglement, questioning how two particles could remain connected over vast distances, seemingly communicating instantaneously without any mediating influences.

Historical experiments such as those conducted by Alain Aspect in the 1980s shifted the discourse surrounding entanglement from philosophical speculation to empirical validation. Aspect's groundbreaking work provided compelling evidence for the correlations predicted by quantum mechanics, illuminating the phenomenon of entanglement through meticulously designed tests that confirmed the non-locality of quantum states. These experiments not only substantiated the predictions of quantum theory but also reignited debates surrounding the interpretation of quantum mechanics and the fundamental nature of reality.

The fabric of contemporary quantum physics is now heavily interwoven with the principles of entanglement, which have given birth to discussions about quantum information theory, quantum teleportation, and emerging technologies such as quantum cryptography and quantum computing. As researchers dive deeper into entanglement's implications, applications that leverage this phenomenon are expanding exponentially. Quantum entanglement has unraveled possibilities for secure communication channels, enabling information to be transmitted in a manner impervious to eavesdropping, a development rooted in the principles of entanglement and the strict limitations of classically transmitted signals.

In the dynamic quest for new technologies and deeper understanding, the historical narrative of entanglement underscores a remarkable journey that reshaped our understanding and interpretation of interactions at the quantum level. It serves as a testament to our profound longing to comprehend the mysteries of the universe, revealing interconnections that transcend the conventional barriers of space and time, ultimately setting the stage for groundbreaking innovations like Quantum Proxy. The implications of entanglement extend beyond mere scientific inquiry; they challenge our philosophical perceptions of existence and human connections in infinite and undefined ways. As we stand on the precipice of utilizing these principles to develop technologies that redefine communication and interaction, the historical evolution of entanglement remains a critical touchstone, guiding our explorations into the realms of possibility where quantum mechanics collides with human experience.

3.2. Einstein's Spooky Action at a Distance

The concept often referred to by Albert Einstein as "spooky action at a distance" illustrates one of the most puzzling and profound aspects of quantum mechanics: entanglement. At the heart of this phenomenon is the realization that particles such as electrons, when entangled, do not retain independent identities in the classical sense. Instead, they become intertwined such that the state of one particle instantaneously affects the state of another, regardless of the spatial separation between them. This intriguing trait raises critical questions about the nature of space, time, and reality, challenging our classical intuitions and underscoring the fundamental principles of quantum physics.

Einstein first introduced this term in response to the implications of quantum entanglement, a discovery that emerged alongside the development of quantum theory in the early 20th century. He, along with his contemporaries, grappled with the unsettling idea that measuring one particle in an entangled pair could instantly influence the outcome for its counterpart, independent of the distance separating them. For instance, if two electrons are entangled and one is measured to be spinning up, the other will instantaneously be determined to be spinning down, even if it is light-years away. This phenomenon contradicts the classical expectation that information cannot travel faster than the speed of light, as stipulated by Einstein's own theory of relativity.

The implications of this entanglement were famously articulated in the Einstein-Podolsky-Rosen (EPR) paper of 1935, which proposed a thought experiment designed to question the completeness of quantum mechanics. The EPR paradox posited that if quantum mechanics were accurate, then two particles could instantaneously affect each other's states, regardless of the distance between them. This conclusion suggested that either the quantum description was incomplete or that particles possess predetermined states before measurement—an assertion fiercely contested by proponents of quantum mechanics, including Niels Bohr.

The term "spooky action" captures the profound philosophical questions that entanglement raises. Does this phenomenon suggest a hidden layer of connections between distant particles? What does it say about our understanding of causality and locality? If entangled particles can influence each other instantaneously, does it imply that the universe is a deeply interconnected fabric, one in which the rules of traditional physics do not apply?

Numerous experiments have since provided empirical validation for entanglement, notably those conducted by Alain Aspect in the 1980s. These experiments tested Bell's Theorem, which formulated a way to distinguish between classical local hidden variable theories and quantum mechanics. Aspect's results demonstrated that measurements on entangled particles were correlated in ways that classical theories could not explain, supporting the quantum perspective and Einstein's skepticism of such non-local interactions.

As we explore the topic further, it becomes essential to grasp the mathematical frameworks that describe entanglement. Entangled states can be represented mathematically through their wave functions, which encode the probabilities of measuring certain properties, such as spin or polarization. The Bell states, for instance, are maximally entangled states that exhibit this characteristic. When described as vectors in a complex probability space, the wave functions for these states showcase the inherent non-local correlations manifesting in entangled particles.

This foundational understanding of entanglement is crucial as we venture into technologic realms that could redefine human interaction through Quantum Proxy. The idea of utilizing entangled particles for instantaneous communication or telepresence prompts both excitement and ethical considerations. If we could harness these properties, the possibilities would extend far beyond mere communication; they could transform the essence of connectedness itself.

Engaging with the implications of spooky action at a distance extends into various practical applications. Quantum cryptography, for instance, leverages entanglement to create unbreakable codes, ensuring secure transmission of information. Similarly, quantum teleportation exploits these principles to transfer quantum states from one particle to another over arbitrary distances, a concept reminiscent of science fiction yet grounded in the principles of quantum mechanics.

The exploration of entanglement prompts us to reconsider our understanding of communication and presence. If instantaneous interaction is achievable, how do we redefine concepts of distance, identity, and interpersonal relationships? The "spooky" characteristics of entanglement, while unsettling, evoke profound insights into the fabric of reality, urging a reevaluation of our place within it.

As we stand on the threshold of potentially utilizing entanglement for innovative technologies like Quantum Proxy, the legacy of Einstein's "spooky action" not only captures the intricacies of quantum mechanics but also illuminates pathways toward applications that could profoundly impact human existence. Embracing the enigmatic nature of quantum entanglement inspires a collective curiosity to explore further, pushing the boundaries of what we deem possible. Thus, understanding this phenomenon is paramount, as it underpins the technologies that may soon allow us to redefine presence and create unprecedented connections across the universe.

3.3. Mathematical Description of Entanglement

Mathematical descriptions of entanglement in quantum mechanics serve as a crucial bridge between abstract theoretical concepts and empirical phenomena that have been meticulously tested in experiments. These mathematical frameworks not only enhance our understanding of the nature of entangled states but also lay the groundwork for potential technological applications in realms such as Quantum Proxy, where instantaneous communication and telepresence may one day become feasible.

At the heart of entanglement lies the tensor product structure found in quantum mechanics. When multiple quantum systems are under consideration, such as two particles or more, their individual states can be combined into a joint state, which lies in a larger Hilbert space. Mathematically, this is represented using the tensor product. For example, if we have two two-level quantum systems (qubits), their states can be expressed as vectors in a two-dimensional complex vector space. The combined system's state is contained in a four-dimensional space formed by the tensor product of the individual qubits' spaces:

$H = H_1 \otimes H_2$, where H_1 and H_2 are the individual state spaces of each qubit.

The intriguing aspect of entangled states is that they cannot be factored into the states of individual particles. For example, the Bell states, which are maximally entangled states, illustrate this non-factorability. The four Bell states can be expressed as follows:

1. $|\Phi^+\rangle = (|00\rangle + |11\rangle)/\sqrt{2}$
2. $|\Phi^-\rangle = (|00\rangle - |11\rangle)/\sqrt{2}$

3. $|\Psi^+\rangle = (|01\rangle + |10\rangle)/\sqrt{2}$
4. $|\Psi^-\rangle = (|01\rangle - |10\rangle)/\sqrt{2}$

Each of these states signifies a particular type of maximum entanglement. When a measurement is performed on one qubit of an entangled pair, the state's wave function collapses, and the correlated outcome appears instantaneously on the other qubit. This phenomenon can be described mathematically through the collapse of the wave function, whereby the act of measurement affects the state of the entire system, reflecting the non-local properties of entanglement highlighted by Einstein's thoughts.

The mathematical description extends beyond pure states to encompass mixed states represented by density matrices, which incorporate probabilities pertaining to various states within a quantum system. The density matrix, ρ, captures the statistical properties of quantum systems, and for an entangled state, the density matrices cannot be expressed as a mere product of the individual systems:

$\rho = |\Psi\rangle\langle\Psi|$,

This formalism becomes especially crucial when discussing entanglement characteristics, particularly the concepts of entanglement entropy and the negativity of the density matrix. These quantifiers provide insights into the extent of entanglement between particles. For instance, the von Neumann entropy $S(\rho)$ and negativity can be used to characterize the amount of entanglement present, offering mathematical tools to quantify how entangled two particles are.

Furthermore, the principles articulated in Bell's theorem introduce a critical lens through which entanglement can be examined. This theorem demonstrates that no local hidden variable theory can replicate the predictions made by quantum mechanics regarding the correlations observed in entangled particles. Bell's inequalities serve as pivotal mathematical constructs that provide empirical tests to distinguish classical physics from quantum mechanics, reinforcing the profound implications arising from entanglement.

Entanglement also finds itself at the heart of quantum teleportation —an application where the state of a quantum system can be transmitted from one location to another without the physical transfer of the system itself. The mathematics underpinning quantum teleportation, utilizing entangled states and classical communication, reveal how information can traverse distances instantaneously, underscoring the entangled nature of quantum systems. The protocol requires shared entangled pairs between two parties, Alice and Bob, alongside classical communication, yielding a successful transmission of quantum states through entanglement.

As researchers continue to explore the mathematical landscapes of entangled systems, the pathways to developing holistic quantum technologies unfold. For instance, crafting better algorithms for quantum cryptography employs intricate entangled states that promise secure communications shielded from eavesdropping. In quantum computing, qubits' entanglements allow for operations that surpass classical computing capabilities, heralding a new wave of technological advancement.

As we gravitate toward the application of these mathematical principles in technologies like Quantum Proxy, where the prospect of real-time telepresence and instantaneous interactions becomes an alluring target, understanding the mathematical structures of entanglement becomes pivotal. The mathematical framework surrounding entangled states provides not just the language for articulating quantum phenomena but also the foundational tools for translating these phenomena into practical applications, thereby redefining human interaction across vast distances in the not-so-distant future. In this paradigm shift, entanglement is not merely a curiosity of quantum physics; it represents a transformative avenue toward reshaping our experience of connection and presence in the universe, illuminating pathways that previously lay dormant in the annals of scientific inquiry. Through advanced mathematical comprehension, the dream of Quantum Proxy becomes tangible, with the potential to connect lives and experiences across the cosmos instantaneously, reshaping our understanding of presence and connection itself.

3.4. Applications Beyond Classical Physics

In the realm of contemporary physics, the implications of quantum mechanics extend far beyond the thoroughly defined laws of classical physics, heralding transformative applications that have the potential to redefine our understanding of communication, interaction, and presence itself. The preceding chapters have meticulously unveiled the fundamentals of quantum mechanics, emphasizing the remarkable phenomena of entanglement and the quantum state, which now serve as the foundation for exploring applications that transcend classical limitations. Within this context, the idea of Quantum Proxy emerges—a visionary concept suggesting that the principles of quantum entanglement can be leveraged to facilitate novel forms of telepresence that resonate with our human experience.

As we probe into applications beyond classical physics, we recognize that while classical mechanics offers a robust framework for understanding macroscopic interactions, it falters in addressing the intricacies of subatomic phenomena. Quantum mechanics challenges the deterministic worldview, introducing concepts such as probability, uncertainty, and non-locality. These unique attributes not only augment the interpretative landscape of reality but also open avenues for groundbreaking technological applications.

One of the most potent applications of quantum mechanics lies in the domain of communication. Traditional communication methods, reliant on classical signals and media, are inherently constrained by the limitations of speed—predominantly that of light—and the physical separation of entities. However, the insights drawn from quantum entanglement suggest a framework where information could be shared instantaneously across vast distances, bringing us closer to the possibility of telepresence. Envision a future where individuals are able to share experiences, emotions, and cognitive interactions as if they were co-located, fundamentally transforming the dynamics of remote interactions.

Considerations of quantum communication technologies, such as quantum key distribution (QKD), exemplify the profound shift from classical approaches. QKD hinges on the principles of entanglement to create unbreakable encryption keys. Information encoded in quantum states can neither be intercepted nor replicated without detection, fostering extraordinary levels of security in data transfer. In this reframed communication paradigm, the potential of utilizing entangled particles for instantaneous communication reshapes not only our technological capabilities but also the sociocultural constructs of presence and connection.

In the realm of telemedicine, applications of Quantum Proxy could revolutionize remote patient monitoring and collaborative healthcare practices. Imagine telepresence technology that allows medical practitioners to engage with patients through instantaneous, immersive communication. Surgeons could advise colleagues in real-time during procedures, providing access to specialized knowledge irrespective of geographical barriers. Quantum entanglement renders the distances effectively meaningless, enabling healthcare systems to function seamlessly across borders and cultures.

Furthermore, the integration of quantum proxies within educational frameworks invites transformative potentials for learning and knowledge dissemination. Students, educators, and experts could collaboratively engage in a shared experiential learning process, overcoming traditional boundaries defined by presence. Envision virtual classrooms where students from diverse backgrounds interact with world-renowned scholars, participating in real-time collaborative projects that blur the lines of distance.

In industrial and manufacturing contexts, Quantum Proxy facilitates innovations in operational efficiency through real-time monitoring and data exchange across supply chains. By fostering instant communication, organizations can dynamically adjust operations to meet fluctuations in demand, manage inventory more effectively, and engage in predictive maintenance across global facilities, improving productivity and minimizing resource waste.

The potential applications of Quantum Proxy stretch into the realms of adventure and exploration as well. In space exploration, for instance, instant communication through quantum entanglement could allow spacecraft to relay data back to Earth instantaneously, fostering improved collaboration among scientists across interplanetary missions. This not only holds implications for advancements in our understanding of the cosmos but the very nature of humanity's relationship with space.

However, profound possibilities heralded by applications beyond classical physics also raise challenging ethical considerations. As the concept of presence is reshaped through technological advancements, questions arise surrounding privacy, consent, and the nature of experience. If telepresence encourages more intimate engagements, how do we navigate the nuances of personal information sharing? The responsibility of ensuring ethical frameworks corresponding to these technologies will emerge as a fundamental design principle as society delves deeper into the quantum landscape.

The implications of these applications extend beyond technology; they penetrate social dynamics and influence cultural interactions. The ability to communicate and connect in real-time, irrespective of distance, has the potential to engender more profound social cohesion and shared experiences among individuals and communities globally. Conversely, it may also amplify existing inequalities in access to technology and information, necessitating concerted efforts to bridge these gaps.

In summary, the applications that arise from delving into quantum mechanics and its principles beckon an era characterized by innovation and connection that transcends the limitations of classical physics. Quantum Proxy encapsulates not just a technological endeavor but a philosophical exploration into the very nature of human connection and understanding. As we confront the formidable challenges of privacy and ethics while pursuing these transformative technologies, it is imperative to engage in meaningful dialogue that encompasses the diverse impacts across cultures, sectors, and communities. The journey ahead promises to challenge our perceptions and redefine what it means to be present in a world where distance becomes merely an afterthought in our interconnected existence.

3.5. Redefining Space and Time

The understanding of space and time has historically been defined through the lens of classical physics, where structures of the universe appear as fixed dimensions governed by Newtonian concepts of absolute time and Euclidean geometry. However, the advent of quantum mechanics and its intricate revelations, particularly through the mechanisms of quantum entanglement and superposition, challenges and redefines these foundational notions. As we venture into the realms illuminated by Quantum Proxy, the application of quantum entanglement offers a profound shift in how we comprehend and utilize the constructs of space and time, suggesting that reality is far more interconnected and fluid than previously imagined.

At the core of this redefinition lies the principle of non-locality—an inherent characteristic of entangled quantum states that suggests interactions can occur without any spatial limitations. When particles become entangled, their states are no longer independent but are intrinsically linked, resulting in correlations that persist regardless of the distance separating them. This prompts a reevaluation of traditional notions of proximity and presence; in the quantum realm, two particles can exist in a shared state, fostering immediate interaction that defies the constraints of classical physics. Essentially, the universe exhibits a cosmic web of connections that transcend spatial separations, fundamentally altering our understanding of how objects can be related in time and space.

The radical implications of this interconnectedness extend into various theoretical frameworks that belong within the ambit of quantum mechanics. For instance, the phenomenon of entanglement implies that our perception of simultaneity could be drastically altered. In a classical context, events are perceived to occur in a linear manner —one after another—bound by a continuous flow of time. However, quantum mechanics, particularly through phenomena such as Bell's theorem, offers a narrative where entangled states indicate that measurements on two distant particles can be correlated instantaneously, suggesting that temporal sequences are not absolute but may vary based on the observer's frame of reference.

This reimagining of time is further bolstered by the principle of superposition, which postulates that quantum systems exist in a multiplicity of states until measured. The act of measurement serves not only as a mechanism to extract information but also as a process that effectively collapses possibilities into singular outcomes. This conceptualization evokes questions regarding the nature of time itself —if potentialities exist simultaneously until an observer engages with the system, does time manifest differently in the quantum domain, perhaps appearing as a fluid entity rather than a rigid sequence?

Within the context of Quantum Proxy, these principles suggest that telepresence—defined as the ability for individuals to project themselves into remote locations, effectively sharing experiential and emotional interactions—could transcend traditional methods of communication. Rather than merely transmitting information in discrete packets with inherent latency, quantum systems utilizing entangled proxies could facilitate instantaneous interactions. This reality implies that more nuanced and authentic exchanges could unfold as if parties were co-located, dissolving the classical boundaries of distance and time.

Imagine scenarios where collaborative workspaces allow teams scattered across the globe to interact in real-time, engaging in problem-solving or creativity as if in the same room. This potential expansion of telepresence challenges not only the physical constructs of space but also the temporal dynamics of interaction—collaboration could occur across vast distances seamlessly, blurring the lines between physical presence and experiential sharing. This may redefine the very essence of community, as individuals experience shared realities that transcend geographical confines.

Furthermore, the implications of redefining space and time extend into realms beyond mere communication, permeating fields such as medicine, education, and space exploration. In healthcare, practitioners could engage with patients across continents, sharing therapeutic experiences and assessments instantaneously. Within educational contexts, students could participate in live classes with world-renowned experts irrespective of their geographic locations, fostering cultural exchange and global collaboration in real-time.

In the universe of quantum mechanics, the once steadfast notions of space and time are unfurled, leading us to a transformative understanding where presence becomes paradoxical. Clarity gives way to fluidity, revealing the interconnectedness of all particles and further illuminating the potential for Quantum Proxy to harness these qualities. By reframing our perceptions, we can venture further into developing technologies that redefine our relational structures, forging depths of connection that were once outside the grasp of our classical understanding.

Importantly, as we stride into these futuristic realms of engagement, we must also grapple with the ethical dilemmas that accompany the fluid nature of space and time within quantum realms. The potential for instant communication introduces substantial considerations regarding privacy, consent, and the implications of redefining interpersonal relationships. Creating ethical frameworks to navigate these concerns will be pivotal in ensuring that the benefits of Quantum Proxy are realized while safeguarding the dignity and autonomy of individuals.

In summary, the redefinition of space and time through the principles of quantum entanglement and superposition invites us into a new era of comprehension and communication. As we explore the potential applications of Quantum Proxy and the technologies it can foster, we immerse ourselves in a world where interactions are not hindered by distance and where temporal constraints dissolve, allowing for richer human experiences. Embracing this shift serves not just to expand technological possibilities but to evolve our very understanding of how we relate to one another across the cosmos. The unfolding journey urges us to consider the profound impacts on humanity, beckoning an era of unprecedented connection and interaction grounded in the extraordinary tapestry of quantum reality.

4. The Quantum Proxy Concept

4.1. Defining Telepresence

In a world increasingly shaped by technology, the notion of telepresence emerges as a powerful beacon of possibility. At its essence, telepresence refers to the ability to create the illusion of being present in a location other than one's actual physical space, enabling users to interact with that environment as though they were there. This phenomenon marries the advancements in virtual and augmented reality technologies with the foundational principles of quantum mechanics, particularly through the concept of Quantum Proxy.

Defining telepresence requires an exploration of its dimensions and implications. It is not limited merely to remote communication via video conferencing or conventional virtual reality environments; instead, it encompasses a multi-layered experience that blurs the boundaries between physical and virtual realms. True telepresence conjures the sensation of being in another place, engaging all senses rather than just sight and sound. This immersion is facilitated through advanced technologies that create highly interactive and realistic simulations, allowing individuals to feel and respond to a shared virtual or augmented environment.

Current applications of telepresence can be seen across various sectors, from corporate environments where virtual meetings have proliferated to social settings such as virtual gatherings or gaming communities. However, most prevalent forms of telepresence are bound by technological limitations, often stymied by latency issues, lack of sensory feedback, and limited emotional engagement. Traditional telepresence technology operates within the frameworks established by classical physics, reliant on lagging signals that inhibit real-time interaction, thus diminishing the effect of true presence.

The advent of Quantum Proxy introduces a paradigm shift in how we perceive and implement telepresence. Leveraging the principles of quantum mechanics, particularly quantum entanglement, Quantum Proxy proposes a mechanism wherein individuals may not just simulate presence, but actualize it through entangled particles that facilitate instantaneous connection and interaction across vast distances. Imagine entering a space and sharing an authentic engagement with others as they touch nearby objects, where the sensory experience feels profoundly real—even if geographically separated by continents.

One critical aspect of telepresence is how it challenges our conventional understanding of space and time. In a standard telepresence experience, users are still confined to their physical environments, limited by geographical and temporal constraints. However, quantum entanglement posits that two entangled particles can operate in an interconnected state, allowing for real-time exchange of information that contravenes classical limitations. Consequently, this suggests that telepresence could extend beyond mere visual and auditory simulations to incorporate haptic feedback, emotional resonance, and an authentic sense of being there—transforming interactions into a shared real-time experience.

In defining telepresence through the lens of Quantum Proxy, several core principles come into play, intricately entwined with the foundational elements of quantum mechanics. The first is the concept of superposition, where quantum systems can exist in multiple states simultaneously. In the context of telepresence, this would enable users to engage with overlapping realities, perceiving and interacting with multiple environments concurrently, ensuring that the experience is richer and more nuanced compared to conventional methods.

The concept of entanglement further elucidates the potential of telepresence, where two or more users can become entangled through their interactions. If individuals could leverage the entangled states of particles, their experiences could become more synchronized despite physical separation, allowing for instantaneous emotional and cognitive exchanges. This non-locality of quantum systems would facilitate a more profound connection among participants, who could exist beyond conventional boundaries of time and space, deepening the quality of relationships forged in virtual environments.

Furthermore, as telepresence technologies evolve, ethical considerations should emerge seamlessly within the framework of their development. Defining what it means to be 'present' in virtual interactions becomes imperative, especially as we harness the capabilities of quantum mechanics to reshape our experiences. The implications of immersive telepresence touch upon issues of privacy, emotional authenticity, and the blurred lines of identity—necessitating meaningful dialogues that address responsibility and inclusivity in the technological pursuit.

In conclusion, defining telepresence transcends mere technological advancement; it invites profound contemplation on presence, connection, and shared experiences. The marriage of telepresence with quantum entanglement offers a glimpse into a future where the boundaries of location dissolve, yielding a world enriched by authentic interactions that transcend spatial limitations. As we stand on the threshold of realizing Quantum Proxy's potential, the journey into redefining telepresence promises to illuminate not just the technological landscape but the very nature of human experience itself. This exploration beckons us forward, inviting us to imagine and ultimately realize a tapestry of interconnected existence, where the relationships we cultivate resonate with authenticity, depth, and immediacy, reshaping the story of how we engage with one another in an ever-evolving world.

4.2. Early Innovations in Telepresence

The concept of telepresence has evolved significantly over the years, fueled by advancements in technology and a deeper understanding of human interaction. Early innovations in telepresence were often rudimentary, limited by the technology of their time, yet they laid the foundation for the transformative potentials we see today. Telepresence, at its core, aims to provide the sensation of being in a different location through various technological means, and while the goal remains the same, the approaches have diversified dramatically.

In the early days, telepresence solutions were largely predicated on audiovisual technology. Pioneering inventions such as the videophone offered a glimpse into remote communication, allowing users to see and hear each other over long distances. Although limited by bandwidth and connection quality, these systems represented a significant leap in how people could interact across space. The videophone, while exciting, was often riddled with issues such as latency and poor image quality, which hampered the feeling of true presence. Users were still acutely aware of the disconnect caused by the physical separation, and awkward pauses or delays could make conversations feel stilted, diminishing the potential for genuine connection.

As the telecommunication landscape evolved, so did the innovations in telepresence. The advent of high-definition video conferencing systems in the late 20th and early 21st centuries marked a transformative moment. Technologies such as teleconferencing bridges and immersive video walls began to create a more lifelike experience for remote meetings. Large multiplexed displays and camera arrays enabled participants to interact as though they were in the same room. Immersive environments aimed to bring together individuals in a three-dimensional space, allowing multiple users to engage in a shared virtual setting. However, even with these innovations, several challenges remained, including the fixed nature of these setups, which required specific locations and lacked mobility.

Parallel to this technologic evolution, advances in virtual and augmented reality began to emerge, opening further possibilities for telepresence experiences. Virtual reality headsets and augmented reality interfaces allowed users to step into immersive environments where they could interact in ways that transcended physical limitations. These systems aimed to create a heightened sense of presence by providing a multi-sensory experience. The gradual development of haptic feedback technologies even introduced the possibility for users to engage with virtual objects, thus fostering richer interactions. Nevertheless, such technologies often faced hurdles with hardware limitations, cost, and complexity, which rendered them less accessible to the general populace.

As researchers and innovators continued exploring ways to enhance telepresence systems, they began considering the underlying principles of quantum mechanics. Quantum theory, with its fascinating phenomena such as entanglement and superposition, suggested a pathway toward realizing telepresence in ways that were previously unimaginable. The integration of quantum principles into telepresence technology opened the door to the concept of Quantum Proxy —a paradigm where the instantaneous sharing of experience and presence could become feasible through the utilization of entangled particles.

However, as we transition from early innovations to the prospects laid out by Quantum Proxy, it is essential to understand the challenges we face. Current telepresence solutions still grapple with issues that quantum technologies have the potential to address, beginning with the constraints imposed by classical physics. The effects of latency, sensory limitations, and economic accessibility in existing systems need to be examined closely. By doing so, we can paint a clearer picture of how early telepresence innovations have paved the way for further explorations into quantum-driven alternatives.

The allure of Quantum Proxy lies in its ability to redefine what it means to be "present." Imagine a world where users can interact with each other and their environment in real-time, regardless of physical distance, facilitated not by cameras and screens, but by the elegant manipulation of quantum states. As we delve deeper into the technological feasibility of Quantum Proxy, we embark on a journey poised to transform the essence of communication, interaction, and ultimately, human connection itself.

4.3. Challenges in Present Telepresence Solutions

The current landscape of telepresence solutions showcases a range of technologies designed to enable remote interaction among individuals. As we dive deeper into the challenges faced by present telepresence systems, it becomes clear that while significant strides have been made, these advancements are entangled with various limitations that hinder the full realization of truly immersive and interactive experiences. Examining these challenges allows us to juxtapose existing capabilities against the transformative potential offered by future technologies, particularly those rooted in quantum mechanics.

One of the most notable challenges in present telepresence solutions is latency. Traditional video conferencing systems are particularly sensitive to network issues, where even minor delays can disrupt the flow of conversation and reduce the natural rhythm of interaction. The lag can lead to overlapping speech, awkward pauses, and a disjointed experience that diminishes the sense of being present. While advancements in broadband technology have improved latency in recent years, there remains a fundamental limitation imposed by the speeds of classical communication methods, which operate under the constraints of electromagnetic signals traveling through physical mediums.

Furthermore, the sensory limitations of current telepresence technologies restrict the depth of engagement possible in virtual interactions. Most telepresence systems focus predominantly on visual and auditory inputs, leaving out tactile sensations, emotional nuances, and other sensory experiences that are integral to human communication. While some systems incorporate basic haptic feedback, the technology lacks the sophistication and realism required to foster a genuine feeling of presence, often leaving users feeling disconnected from the environment and the people they are engaging with.

The physical setup required for many telepresence systems adds another layer of complexity and challenge. Conventional setups often involve expensive equipment and specific configurations, such as multiple screens, sophisticated camera systems, and ample bandwidth, making them less accessible for widespread adoption. The infrastructure required to support high-quality telepresence can be a barrier for smaller organizations or individuals who seek to utilize these technologies for personal or professional purposes.

In addressing these limitations, it is essential to consider not only the technological hurdles but also the ethical implications of the existing telepresence solutions. Issues surrounding privacy and data security persist—a significant concern when information is transmitted over networks. Current telepresence systems must navigate potential vulnerabilities that could expose sensitive information during live interactions. Additionally, ethical considerations arise when examining the potential for socio-economic divides that may deepen as access to advanced telepresence technologies remains unequal.

Integrating and synchronizing these telepresence technologies with existing communication platforms poses another challenge. Many organizations employ a patchwork of tools and services to communicate effectively. Seamlessly blending these systems with new telepresence innovations requires not only technological compatibility but also organizational buy-in and training to ensure users can leverage enhanced capabilities.

As we assess the lessons learned from present telepresence solutions, we gain insight into how emerging technologies can address these hurdles. The prospect of Quantum Proxy technology, built upon the principles of quantum entanglement, offers an enticing alternative. Quantum systems could potentially overcome latency issues by instantaneously transmitting information across entangled particles, thereby facilitating real-time interactions that are unencumbered by the constraints of classical communication. Additionally, leveraging quantum principles could enable rich, immersive engagement experiences that fully replicate the nuances of in-person interactions.

Moreover, Quantum Proxy technology could redefine accessibility in telepresence solutions, reducing the infrastructure costs associated with high-quality video and audio systems. Embracing such advances could pave the way for more widespread adoption across various demographics, breaking down barriers that currently limit engagement in remote communication.

In summary, while present telepresence solutions reflect substantial progress in fostering remote interactions, they are marred by challenges stemming from latency, sensory limitations, accessibility, and ethical concerns. Addressing these challenges necessitates innovation that transcends current capabilities and encourages holistic approaches to enhancing remote communication. Quantum Proxy technology stands at the forefront of this innovation wave, with the potential to reshape how we connect and interact across vast distances, transforming the landscape of telepresence beyond traditional limitations. As we look forward to integrating quantum principles into telepresence, the challenge remains to not only improve technology but also to ensure it serves the broader goals of inclusivity, authenticity, and human connection in our increasingly digital world.

4.4. Imagining Quantum Proxy Technology

Imagining Quantum Proxy Technology invites us to explore the potential paradigms of interaction facilitated by quantum mechanics, particularly through the concept of telepresence. As the frontier of technology continuously advances, the notion of being able to project oneself into another location instantaneously becomes increasingly tantalizing when viewed through the lens of quantum entanglement. Quantum Proxy posits a world where distance loses its significance, allowing experiences to unfold in real-time across vast expanses of space.

At the core of Quantum Proxy technology is the unique property of quantum entanglement. When two or more particles become entangled, their states are interlinked, such that the measurement of one particle's state instantaneously determines the state of the other, irrespective of the distance separating them. This phenomenon presents an opportunity to forge connections that defy the constraints imposed by classical physics, reshaping our understanding of presence.

Imagine a world where families separated by oceans can gather in an immersive virtual setting, sharing laughter and conversation as if they were in the same room. This is more than mere video conferencing; it is a truly engaged experience, where every nuance of interaction is preserved. Quantum Proxy could leverage entangled states to enable individuals to feel the warmth of a loved one, sense their reactions, and share in moments of joy and consolation. By harnessing these quantum principles, we can envision telepresence that resonates with authenticity and emotional depth, redefining how we interact across digital landscapes.

Additionally, envision the application of Quantum Proxy technology within the enterprise sector. Companies could utilize quantum entanglement for international collaborations, allowing teams in disparate locations to engage in strategic decision-making in real-time. As decisions unfold instantaneously, organizations could maintain agility and seamless communication, propelling productivity to new heights. Imagine working in a conference room that feels as if every colleague is present, exchanging ideas as freely as if they were physically sharing the space, thus fostering innovation and collaboration.

In education, Quantum Proxy could revolutionize how knowledge is transferred and expertise shared. Students could attend lectures delivered by experts, participate in workshops, and engage with peers from across the globe as if they were all congregated in a physical learning environment. The experience would not solely be visual but tactile, allowing students to manipulate virtual materials or participate in experiments collaboratively, thus fostering engagement and curiosity in learning.

Space exploration also holds promising possibilities for Quantum Proxy. Imagine astronauts aboard a spacecraft being able to maintain real-time connections with scientists on Earth, sharing their experiences, receiving insights, and collaborating on problem-solving without the delays currently imposed by the vast distances of outer space. Such instantaneous data transfer could fundamentally alter the dynamics of space missions, enhancing the success and safety of exploratory initiatives.

However, imagining such technology also necessitates acknowledging the challenges and implications it raises. The ability to project oneself into another space is not without ethical ramifications. Considerations related to privacy and data security must be paramount as we develop quantum technologies that allow for deeper immersion and interaction. As information is transacted instantaneously, safeguarding sensitive data and ensuring that individuals maintain control over their virtual presence will become critical.

Moreover, the passion for innovation should be balanced with awareness of accessibility. As Quantum Proxy emerges, efforts must be made to ensure that this technology does not deepen existing inequalities. Access to advanced technologies must be democratized, enabling all segments of society to participate in and benefit from such unprecedented advancements.

Envisioning Quantum Proxy technology involves reconciling these exhilarating potentials with the ethical frameworks necessary to guide its development. As we rapidly approach an era where quantum mechanics can offer groundbreaking advantages in communication, we must engage in collective dialogue about what presence means in our increasingly interconnected world. The pursuit of quantum-driven telepresence offers unprecedented opportunities to amplify human connection while inviting us to consider the responsibilities that accompany such capabilities.

In conclusion, the imagination surrounding Quantum Proxy technology is a vivid tapestry woven with threads of possibility and nuanced consideration. It invites exploration of redefined interactions across various domains, from personal relationships to professional enterprises. As we endeavor to bring this vision into reality, embracing the principles of quantum mechanics as a means to connect and share experiences will undoubtedly transform our lives. The journey ahead urges us to navigate the complexities of this innovation landscape, ensuring that the fruits of quantum technology serve to enrich our humanity and create a world where connection knows no bounds.

4.5. Theoretical Framework and Models

The theoretical framework and models underpinning Quantum Proxy draw extensively from the principles of quantum mechanics, laying the groundwork for understanding how quantum entanglement can facilitate telepresence. This subchapter encapsulates the theoretical constructs that inform Quantum Proxy, its potential applications, and the relevant scientific models that illustrate how these principles can be implemented in practice.

To begin, it is essential to acknowledge that the foundation of quantum mechanics is inherently counterintuitive, challenging classical physics' perceptions of reality. The pivotal principles such as superposition, entanglement, and the wave-particle duality serve as cornerstones for distilling the essence of Quantum Proxy. Quantum entanglement, for instance, describes a scenario where pairs of particles become entangled such that the state of one particle is interconnected with the state of another, irrespective of the distance between them. This means that the measurement of one particle can instantaneously affect the other, a phenomenon that lies at the heart of developing telepresence capabilities.

Additionally, the mathematical description of quantum states through wave functions provides a robust framework for envisioning how such technologies might function in practice. Entangled states can be represented mathematically to explore their properties further, allowing researchers to understand how controlled manipulations can produce measurable outcomes conducive to telepresence applications. The Bell states, representing maximally entangled states, distinguish between different degrees of entanglement and offer rich data that can be exploited to create the desired connectedness that defines telepresence.

Another significant aspect of the theoretical framework is based on modeling scenarios where quantum communication systems operate. These systems leverage techniques such as quantum key distribution (QKD) to ensure secure communication using entangled particles. By creating pairs of entangled photons that can be distributed to multiple locations, researchers can effectively measure the correlations between individual particles to establish secure transmission pathways. The underlying models of QKD utilize quantum mechanics' intrinsic qualities, reinforcing the advantages of using quantum technologies for reliable, real-time communication.

Moreover, various models, such as the quantum teleportation framework, illustrate the feasibility of transmitting quantum states instantaneously through entangled particles, embodying the capabilities anticipated from Quantum Proxy technologies. The process of quantum teleportation, for instance, involves the transfer of quantum information from one location to another without physical movement of the particle itself, utilizing classical communication to achieve this seamless transfer over quantum entanglement.

An important piece of this theoretical puzzle lies in the exploration of quantum networking models, where nodes interconnect utilizing quantum principles to ensure coherent communication channels. In such networks, the entangled quantum states form the basis for establishing connections between various points, facilitating secure and instantaneous data transfer that would not be possible through classical networking methods. This represents a significant leap in how we understand communication technology, ushering in the Quantum Internet—a network based on quantum mechanics principles.

Furthermore, the theoretical models rooted in quantum mechanics extend into discussions surrounding the limitations and challenges inherent in achieving practical applications. Understanding how to mitigate decoherence, a phenomenon that disrupts quantum states, is crucial to maintaining the integrity of entangled particles over extended periods. Existing models in quantum decoherence provide insights into strategies for isolating quantum systems from their environments, thus enhancing the prospects of robust telepresence technologies.

In addition, ethical and philosophical implications emerge when considering the practical application of these theoretical frameworks.

The ramifications of achieving seamless telepresence through quantum technologies compel us to reflect on the nature of presence, identity, and human interaction. Understanding these dynamics is essential in addressing the responsibilities that accompany emerging technologies, promoting dialogue on potential societal impacts as Quantum Proxy technologies become more integrated into everyday life.

In conclusion, the theoretical framework and models underpinning Quantum Proxy weave together principles from quantum mechanics, mathematical representations of quantum states, and the exploration of practical communication scenarios. As we navigate this landscape, it is essential to remain engaged with both the scientific possibilities and the broader implications of bringing such transformative technologies to fruition. The journey is one of discovery, innovation, and responsibility, where the interplay of theory and application informs a future where teleportation of experience and presence may become a remarkable reality, reshaping not just how we communicate, but how we understand our connections with one another across time and space.

5. Quantum Proxy Technological Feasibility

5.1. Quantum Mechanics in Real-world Applications

The growing confluence of quantum mechanics and technology has generated a plethora of real-world applications, signaling profound shifts in various fields that stretch far beyond theoretical frameworks. As we explore quantum mechanics in real-world scenarios, we witness a fascinating interplay between scientific advancement and practical applicability, with remarkable implications for areas ranging from communication to healthcare, manufacturing, and beyond. Quantum Proxy, the potential realization of telepresence through quantum entanglement, epitomizes this transformative surge, leading us to rethink how we engage with the world around us.

One of the most striking implementations of quantum mechanics is seen in the burgeoning field of quantum communication. Traditional forms of communication primarily rely on the propagation of classical signals, which are subject to limitations inherent to transmission speed and interference. Quantum communication, in stark contrast, leverages the unique properties of quantum states—particularly entanglement and superposition—to facilitate instantaneous and secure data transmission. Techniques such as Quantum Key Distribution (QKD) utilize entangled particles to create secure encryption methods that render traditional hacking attempts futile. By manipulating entangled photons, users can create encryption keys shared between parties that are physically impossible to duplicate without detection. This advancement underscores the broader applications of quantum mechanics in ensuring data integrity and privacy in an increasingly digital world.

In addition to enhancing communication security, quantum mechanics is poised to revolutionize industries such as healthcare. The application of quantum technologies in medical imaging, for instance, promises to yield higher resolution images at unprecedented speeds, allowing for earlier detection and more effective treatment of various conditions. Advanced quantum algorithms could analyze vast datasets derived from genomic research or epidemiological studies, thereby driving a new era of personalized medicine where treatments are tailored to individual patients based on their unique genetic makeup.

Moreover, the integration of quantum sensors in medical diagnostics exemplifies a new frontier in patient care. These sensors, leveraging the sensitivity of quantum states to external influences, could detect subtle changes in biological markers, empowering healthcare practitioners with rich insights into patient health that were previously unattainable. As quantum mechanics aligns with biotechnology, the potential for breakthroughs in early diagnosis and individualized treatments demonstrates a significant real-world impact birthed from quantum principles.

The industrial field is also on the cusp of transformation due to the applications of quantum mechanics in manufacturing. Quantum computing promises to optimize production processes and supply chain management through enhanced predictive analytics powered by the unique computational capabilities of quantum systems. The complex calculations required for efficient resource allocation and scheduling, particularly in sprawling industrial environments, can become streamlined to levels previously deemed impossible with classical computers. Consequently, the quantum approach could reduce waste, enhance productivity, and bolster sustainability efforts.

In the arena of space exploration, employing quantum technologies opens prospects for real-time communication across astronomical distances. Quantum entanglement could facilitate instantaneous data relay from spacecraft to mission control, eliminating the time constraints imposed by the speed of light. This capability could enhance safety for astronauts on long-term missions, initiating a new chapter where human presence in space is complemented by seamless interactions with Earth-based teams, ensuring collaborative problem-solving without delays.

However, as we delve into the applicability of quantum mechanics in real-world contexts, the technical barriers present considerable challenges. Overcoming these limitations requires deep interdisciplinary collaboration among physicists, engineers, and industry specialists. The coherence of quantum states is notoriously delicate; maintaining entanglement over long distances remains a paramount challenge that must be addressed for broad-scale implementation of quantum technologies.

To bridge this gap, researchers are exploring a range of solutions, including the development of robust error correction algorithms capable of preserving quantum information in the face of environmental disturbance. Furthermore, integrating existing classical infrastructures with quantum components paves the way to a hybrid landscape where quantum technologies augment traditional systems while the full realization of a quantum-centric world unfolds.

Notably, there are several case studies emerging that showcase the potential of quantum mechanics in practical applications. Organizations such as IBM, Google, and D-Wave Systems are pioneering work in quantum computing, sparking industry collaborations aimed at developing quantum applications that prioritize efficiency and scalability. These initiatives serve as test beds for exploring how quantum mechanics can intersect with existing technologies, facilitating new products and services that leverage quantum capabilities.

In conclusion, the exploration of quantum mechanics in real-world applications exemplifies the substantial impact this field can have across diverse sectors. By harnessing the nuances of entanglement, superposition, and non-locality, we encounter a myriad of possibilities that challenge our current technological paradigms. As we embrace advancements such as Quantum Proxy, we find ourselves at the juncture of profound transformation—where communication, healthcare, manufacturing, and scientific inquiry converge under the auspices of quantum principles, redefining the very fabric of existence in our increasingly interconnected world. The journey into quantum applications compels us to remain vigilant regarding the challenges faced, yet it also invites us to envision a future where human experiences are augmented and enriched through the lens of quantum mechanics, heralding innovations yet to be imagined.

5.2. Current Technological Landscape

In today's rapidly evolving technological landscape, we find ourselves at a crossroads where quantum mechanics increasingly intersects with practical applications, heralding a new era defined by unprecedented capabilities. The last decade has seen significant advancements in various fields, laying the groundwork for potentially transformative technologies, particularly in the realm of quantum communication and, specifically, the concept of Quantum Proxy. As we delve into the current technological landscape, it is important to highlight how the theoretical underpinnings of quantum mechanics are being translated into tangible benefits, thus altering our understanding of presence, communication, and interaction.

The ongoing development of quantum technologies has led to enhancements in computational power, secure communication systems, and sophisticated scientific measurement techniques. Quantum computing, for instance, has witnessed remarkable progress, with organizations like IBM and Google pioneering efforts to create scalable quantum processors capable of performing complex computations that are intractable for classical computers. These advancements showcase the potential for quantum algorithms to revolutionize sectors such as cryptography, optimization, and materials science, proving that the power of quantum mechanics is being harnessed for practical use.

In parallel, the field of quantum communication has emerged as a focal point of innovation. The principles of quantum superposition and entanglement enable the creation of communication channels that come with inherent security features unattainable by classical means. For instance, Quantum Key Distribution (QKD) utilizes entangled particles to ensure that any attempt at eavesdropping is impossible without being detected. This capability not only fortifies cybersecurity measures against growing threats but also highlights the shifting paradigms concerning how we think about communication in an increasingly interconnected world.

Within this context, Quantum Proxy emerges as an exciting possibility that extends beyond mere information transfer. By leveraging entangled states, the concept envisions a future where individuals can interact in real-time, immersing themselves in experiences that feel genuinely present, regardless of their physical locations. This would transform not only interpersonal interactions but also business practices, education, and entertainment, as people share in experiences that are rich with authenticity and emotional resonance. The technology underlying Quantum Proxy has the potential to redefine our perception of distance, presence, and connection through quantum-enhanced telepresence.

Moreover, current technological frameworks are laying foundational pathways for integrating Quantum Proxy within existing systems. The compatibility of quantum technologies with classical infrastructures is a crucial consideration for widespread adoption. As researchers work towards addressing the challenges associated with quantum coherence, error correction, and scalability, the potential for seamless integration becomes increasingly viable. By bridging quantum systems with contemporary communication networks, we can hope to forge a practical realization of Quantum Proxy that combines the best of both worlds.

However, the journey towards fully realizing this transformative concept is not without its obstacles. There are numerous technological barriers to overcome, including issues of decoherence, which disrupt quantum states and hinder their reliability over time. Researchers are diligently exploring ways to mitigate these challenges, drawing from interdisciplinary knowledge in materials science, engineering, and information theory, in order to create robust quantum systems capable of sustained entanglement.

Excitingly, numerous case studies and prototypes are emerging that encapsulate the potential of quantum communication technologies.

From universities conducting quantum teleportation experiments to private companies developing quantum encryption solutions, these initiatives validate the transformative promise of quantum-based applications. Some are already exploring Quantum Proxy concepts, testing how entangled particles can enable more interactive and immersive telepresence experiences, thus demonstrating the technology's potential to reshape communication fundamentally.

Given the profound implications of these advancements, it becomes imperative to simultaneously consider the ethical dimensions surrounding the deployment of quantum technologies. The privacy and surveillance concerns inherent in telepresence capabilities raise critical questions that demand careful navigation. Additionally, issues of equity and access must be addressed to ensure that the benefits of such transformative innovations reach diverse populations, avoiding the entrenchment of existing disparities.

In conclusion, the current technological landscape illustrates an exciting convergence of quantum mechanics and pragmatic application, positioning us at a threshold rich with possibility. The development of Quantum Proxy represents not merely an extension of existing technologies but a fundamentally different approach to communication, offering the tantalizing potential for real-time interactions devoid of physical or temporal constraints. As we explore the implications and possibilities guaranteed by this quantum-driven future, we must remain vigilant about the challenges we face while celebrating the extraordinary opportunities for innovation, connection, and human experience that lie ahead. Embracing this convergence promises to catalyze a reimagining of our relationships with technology and one another, ultimately redefining what it means to connect in an increasingly complex and interlinked world.

5.3. Potential for Integration with Existing Systems

The potential for integration with existing systems is a crucial consideration as we explore the implementation of Quantum Proxy technology—a groundbreaking approach to telepresence grounded in the principles of quantum mechanics, particularly quantum entanglement. As we stand on the threshold of transforming the way we communicate and interact, understanding the pathways to seamlessly integrate this innovative technology into current infrastructures becomes essential. This integration is not merely a technical challenge; it involves strategic thinking, collaboration, and a forward-looking outlook to embrace the unique characteristics of quantum systems while harmonizing them with established communication modalities.

To begin with, the existing technological landscape is predominantly shaped by classical communication networks, encompassing various protocols, hardware systems, and software applications designed for information transmission. Integrating Quantum Proxy technology demands a multifaceted approach that encompasses the adaptation of these classical systems to accommodate quantum principles. For instance, while classical systems rely on electrical signals and electromagnetic waves for communication, Quantum Proxy posits that entangled particles can convey information instantaneously, effectively bypassing the limitations of speed imposed by traditional media. This fundamental difference necessitates the development of quantum communication protocols that can work in tandem with conventional infrastructure.

One pivotal aspect of achieving integration is creating hybrid systems that combine classical and quantum technologies. Researchers and engineers are exploring methods for establishing links between existing communication networks and quantum channels. Such hybrid systems may involve leveraging classical communication methods for initial data exchange while employing quantum entanglement for secure transmission of sensitive information or facilitating richer interactive experiences. For example, a classic streaming video chat could be enhanced using quantum channels to particularly secure the data being shared without compromising the user experience.

Moreover, the challenges posed by the current systems' bandwidth requirements and latency issues necessitate innovative solutions that balance the sophisticated demands of quantum communication with the established expectations of users. While Quantum Proxy technology offers the promise of instantaneity, it must be effectively paired with classical systems that can manage higher data capacities and facilitate smooth interoperability. This convergence invites opportunities for inventive engineering adaptations, where classical infrastructure may serve as a flexible backbone to support emerging quantum channels.

As we envision the future of Quantum Proxy and its integration with existing systems, the role of education and training cannot be understated. Stakeholders—from developers and engineers to users —must be equipped with a foundational understanding of quantum mechanics to adapt to this new paradigm effectively. The complexity inherent in quantum systems necessitates that those involved in the integration process are well-versed in its principles and capable of navigating the nuances that arise from combining different communication modalities. Educational initiatives could undergo a renaissance to include courses tailored for professionals seeking to converge quantum mechanics with their respective fields, fostering a more profound grasp of the technology and its applications.

Collaboration between academia, industry, and government agencies is another vital ingredient in this integration process. By pooling expertise, resources, and insights, these entities can collectively drive research and development efforts that span the conceptualization, prototyping, and deployment of Quantum Proxy technologies. Joint initiatives can pave the way for pilot projects, enabling stakeholders to assess the feasibility and effectiveness of integrating quantum capabilities within existing communication systems before scaling them for broader use. These pilot projects can be instrumental in identifying potential pitfalls and refining approaches based on empirical evidence, leading to more informed decision-making regarding integration processes.

The ethical and regulatory considerations associated with such a transformative leap warrant careful attention as well. The deployment of quantum networks introduces questions of privacy, security, and the socio-economic implications of utilizing such advanced technology. Ensuring that the benefits of integration extend across all demographics will require policies focused on access and inclusivity. The development of regulatory frameworks that govern the safe and equitable use of Quantum Proxy technologies is critical to balancing innovation with responsible stewardship.

Finally, consider the potential impact such integration could have on greater societal implications. Harnessing Quantum Proxy technology could redefine communication norms, facilitating deeper connections among individuals, communities, and organizations as they interact across borders unhindered by time and space constraints. This interconnected global society could inspire novel cultural exchanges, collaborative problem-solving, and an enriched sense of belonging, transforming the landscape of human interaction.

In summary, the potential for integration with existing systems represents a rich terrain for exploration as Quantum Proxy evolves from a concept into a reality. By fostering hybrid approaches, engaging in collaborative endeavors, prioritizing education, and addressing ethical considerations, we can build a bridge between the quantum and classical worlds. The journey towards integrating Quantum Proxy technology is framed not solely as a technological challenge but as an opportunity to redefine human connection and communication, paving the way for a future where distance and isolation fade into the backdrop of a more interconnected existence.

5.4. Overcoming Technological Barriers

In the pursuit of transforming the ambitious concept of Quantum Proxy into a practical reality, we encounter a myriad of technological barriers that must be acknowledged and addressed. These barriers span various dimensions, including the inherent complexities of quantum mechanics, engineering challenges associated with the manipulation and measurement of quantum states, and the integration of new quantum technologies into existing communication frameworks.

One of the foremost challenges lies in maintaining the delicate nature of quantum states. Quantum entanglement, which serves as the foundation for Quantum Proxy, is notoriously fragile. External disturbances, such as environmental noise or interaction with other particles, can lead to decoherence—the process by which entangled states lose their quantum properties and effectively cease to exist. This necessitates the development of robust techniques to isolate quantum systems from their surroundings while preserving coherence over time. Researchers are actively exploring methods such as cryogenic cooling, electromagnetic shielding, and the use of lab-grown materials that minimize decoherence, but practical implementations remain an ongoing area of investigation.

Another significant barrier is the limitation of quantum communication distances. Quantum entanglement operates under the principle that paired particles remain correlated regardless of distance, yet practically establishing and maintaining that entanglement over long distances presents a complex challenge. As entangled pairs are generated, the fidelity of entanglement diminishes with distance due to factors like photon scattering in optical fibers or atmospheric turbulence in free-space transmission. Solutions such as quantum repeaters are being proposed, which could extend the range of entangled communication by using intermediate entangled pairs to relay information over greater distances. However, achieving seamless function in real-world conditions remains a technical hurdle.

Additionally, the current infrastructure of classical communication systems poses another obstacle. While quantum communication technologies demonstrate the potential for instantaneous and secure information transfer, integrating them with the extensive network of classical systems already in place requires significant advancements. The development of protocols that allow quantum and classical systems to operate cohesively is paramount for transitioning Quantum Proxy technology from a theoretical framework to practical applications. Researchers must bridge the gap between quantum communication systems and traditional networking, necessitating innovations in how data packets are transmitted and managed.

The scalability of quantum technologies is another crucial concern. Most current experiments operate in highly controlled laboratory conditions and involve a small number of qubits or entangled particles. To develop Quantum Proxy at a scale where it can be utilized in everyday communication and telepresence applications, advancements in scalability must be prioritized. This will require creating systems that can manage large entangled networks, possibly like a future Quantum Internet, enabling vast numbers of users to connect. Meeting these challenges will demand interdisciplinary collaboration across fields including physics, engineering, computer science, and materials science.

Moreover, as Quantum Proxy systems are developed, the question of accessibility becomes increasingly critical. Current quantum technologies are resource-intensive, requiring specialized knowledge and substantial funding that may create barriers for broad implementation. Ensuring equitable access to these advanced technologies must be a guiding principle as we work towards integrating Quantum Proxy into various sectors of society. It is crucial that efforts are made to democratize access to quantum innovations, permitting a wider array of individuals and communities to benefit from advancements in telepresence and communication.

In tandem with addressing these technological barriers, ethical considerations will also play a critical role in shaping the development of Quantum Proxy. As we extend our capabilities to redefine presence and interaction, questions around privacy, surveillance, and the potential misuse of such technologies must be actively engaged. It is imperative to develop robust ethical frameworks and regulations governing the use of quantum communication technologies, ensuring responsible use while balancing innovation and societal impact.

Finally, the collective drive to overcome these technological barriers is fueled by the immense potential of Quantum Proxy to transform our understanding of connection and interaction. The promise of instantaneous, immersive communication, where distance becomes irrelevant, encapsulates a vision of interconnectedness that could redefine human experiences. As these challenges are addressed, we find ourselves on the precipice of not just technological advancement but a revolution in how we perceive presence in an increasingly interconnected world.

In summary, overcoming the technological barriers associated with Quantum Proxy requires a multifaceted approach that encompasses scientific innovation, ethical engagement, and accessibility consider-ations. The journey ahead is one of discovery, collaboration, and purposeful exploration, challenging us to bring forth a future where quantum principles empower a new era of communication and human connection—one that was once confined to the realm of imagination. The convergence of these efforts stands to reshape the interaction landscape, encouraging a way of being that transcends the limitations of time and space while fostering richer, more meaningful relationships in our lives.

5.5. Case Studies and Prototypes

In the exploration of transformative technologies, case studies and prototypes serve as essential touchstones that illuminate the practical feasibility and innovative potential of concepts like Quantum Proxy. These tangible representations of quantum principles in action offer a concrete understanding of how theoretical underpinnings can trans-late into real-world applications, shaping our future interactions.

One significant case study involves a collaborative project between prestigious research institutions focused on developing a prototype quantum communication network. Researchers aimed to create a secure quantum key distribution (QKD) system defined by entan-gled particles. QKD has been extensively studied as an effective method to safeguard communications against eavesdropping. This specific project utilized entangled photon pairs generated through spontaneous parametric down-conversion. By deploying fiber optic networks interspersed with entanglement swapping techniques, the research team demonstrated that quantum keys could be securely transmitted over significant distances without the risk of interception

—an achievement that illustrates the viability of quantum communication networks as a foundation for Quantum Proxy.

Another prototype example stemmed from the realm of quantum teleportation demonstrations. Researchers at several leading universities successfully demonstrated the transmission of quantum states from one location to another. One highly publicized experiment involved teleporting the quantum state of a photon over a distance of more than ten kilometers. This prototype built on the principles of entanglement and showed great promise for future applications in Quantum Proxy by enabling the transmission of complex quantum information instantaneously. By showcasing the capacity for remote quantum state transfer, this work creates a framework for future advancements in telepresence.

Investigative efforts into quantum sensors also provide vital prototypes that establish the practicality of quantum principles in everyday contexts. Quantum sensors leverage the extreme sensitivity of quantum states to measure physical quantities, such as magnetic fields and gravitational waves. A notable example is the development of atomic magnetometers that utilize entangled atoms to achieve precision that surpasses classical instruments. While primarily aimed at applications ranging from medical imaging to geological exploration, these developments highlight significant opportunities for future integration of quantum sensing technologies within telepresence systems, offering enhanced real-time feedback and immersive experiences.

In the area of education and training, a pioneering project developed an interactive learning platform utilizing virtual reality combined with quantum entanglement principles. Students engaged in experiments to manipulate entangled particles in simulated environments, providing an experiential understanding of quantum concepts. This prototype equips students with immersive learning experiences that foster comprehension of complex quantum mechanics while simultaneously introducing elements of telepresence. Such educational frameworks demonstrate how Quantum Proxy could revolutionize engagement in scientific learning, helping bridge theoretical knowledge with practical application.

Prototypes in the field of quantum computing have also illuminated significant advancements toward realizing Quantum Proxy. Companies like IBM and Google have been at the forefront of developing quantum processors, leading to breakthroughs in computational capabilities. An illustrative case study is IBM's work on its IBM Quantum Experience platform, which allows users to access quantum computers and experiment with quantum algorithms via cloud-based technologies. While this approach is primarily computational, it sets the stage for future telepresence where processing power enables instantaneous sharing of quantum-enhanced experiences, much like what Quantum Proxy envisions.

Furthermore, international collaborations aimed at quantum communication networks have gained momentum, with prototypes being deployed along major cities through initiatives such as the Quantum Internet Alliance. These experimental networks capture the essence of how quantum entanglement can be employed for robust communication systems across urban environments. The successful integration of entangled quantum channels over existing infrastructures represents a substantial step towards implementing Quantum Proxy technology in everyday human interactions.

However, the transition from prototype to widespread application faces challenges that require mitigation. Issues of coherence preservation, scalability, and compatibility with classical systems remain focal points. Research efforts continue to address these challenges, focusing on refining prototypes and optimizing their functionalities to ensure real-world feasibility. Ongoing developments necessitate interdisciplinary collaborations—engineering teams partnering with physicists, technologists, and industry stakeholders to foster a holistic understanding of quantum principles while enhancing functionality.

In conclusion, the compilation of case studies and prototypes represents a crucial conduit for translating theoretical quantum concepts into practical applications. As the principles of quantum communication, entanglement, and teleportation converge with prototypes that showcase their capabilities, the path to realizing Quantum Proxy becomes progressively clearer. Lessons learned from these initial explorations underscore the continued necessity to bridge research with application, enabling a future characterized by seamless telepresence and redefined human experiences. As we unravel the complexities of quantum reality through prototypes, we unlock a transformative potential that holds promise for reshaping communication and interaction in an interconnected world.

6. Breaking Down Quantum Communication

6.1. Principles of Quantum Communication

The principles of quantum communication are underpinned by some of the most profound and counterintuitive concepts within quantum mechanics. As we navigate the fascinating landscape of Quantum Proxy, understanding these principles is essential, especially as they relate to the potential for instantaneous telepresence and transformative communication technologies.

At the foundation of quantum communication resides the principle of superposition. This principle postulates that a quantum system can exist in multiple states simultaneously until a measurement is made. For instance, a qubit, the basic unit of quantum information, can represent both 0 and 1 at the same time, expanding the computing power beyond classical binary conditions. This multiplicative character of quantum bits allows for a more complex and rich structure of information encoding, setting the stage for developing quantum communication protocols that are far more powerful than classical counterparts.

Closely intertwined with superposition is the concept of quantum entanglement, the phenomenon wherein particles become linked in such a way that the state of one instantly affects the state of another, regardless of the distance separating them. This feature enables correlations that can be used for transmitting information securely. When entangled particles are measured, the outcome for one particle predicts the outcome for its partner. This non-locality property serves as the cornerstone for quantum communication technologies, facilitating immediate information relay that transcends classical limitations.

Quantum Key Distribution (QKD) is one of the most celebrated applications of these principles. It employs quantum mechanics to create secure communication channels, ensuring that any attempt to eavesdrop can be detected by legitimate parties. Using entangled particles, QKD allows individuals to share keys used to encrypt their communication effectively. If an eavesdropper attempts to intercept the quantum states, the disturbance created will be observable, alerting users to potential breaches. This key aspect of quantum communication offers security that is provably assured by the laws of physics rather than merely the complexity of encryption algorithms.

The capabilities offered by quantum communication begin to stand out when we compare them with classical communication methods. Classical communication systems operate under assumptions of deterministic pathways, where signals are sent through defined mediums subject to interference and loss. Quantum systems, however, challenge these norms by utilizing quantum entanglement to create secure, instantaneous communication channels that hold the promise of facilitating rich interactions without the latency typically associated with classical methods. This quantum leap allows for secure channels that do not rely on the traditional encryption methods that can be vulnerable to sophisticated attacks.

Looking to the future, the potential for innovations in quantum communication technology appears boundless. Advancements in quantum repeaters may enable the extension of entangled communication over long distances without significant loss of information. These repeaters effectively bridge gaps to create a "Quantum Internet," allowing entangled states to be preserved and manipulated across networks, fostering secure and instantaneous communication on a global scale. Moreover, as quantum techniques are further integrated into existing systems, we could see a paradigm shift in how humans interact with technology, mood, and presence.

The future possibilities of quantum communication are endless. Imagine an interconnected world where not only messages but entire experiences can be shared seamlessly. Virtual meetings would evolve into immersive experiences, allowing individuals to 'be' at a location while interacting as if physically present. Research on scalable quantum architectures and the exploration of quantum mesh networks augur well for realizing this vision. The landscape of communication and connectivity could transform dramatically, leading to innovative applications that rethink interpersonal interactions.

In conclusion, the principles of quantum communication offer a profound understanding of how entanglement and superposition create opportunities for next-generation technologies. The framework established through quantum principles not only enhances security and efficiency but also heralds a transformative shift in how we comprehend and experience communication. As Quantum Proxy promises a new era defined by its applications, it beckons us toward a future where instant presence and interaction become an integral part of our interconnected existence.

6.2. Quantum Key Distribution

In the realm of contemporary communication, quantum key distribution (QKD) stands out as a particularly promising application of the principles of quantum mechanics, specifically leveraging the phenomena of entanglement and superposition to offer unparalleled security in data transmission. This technology significantly shifts the dynamics of how we think about secure communication, fundamentally redefining our understanding of privacy and security in a digital age increasingly fraught with cybersecurity threats.

QKD fundamentally capitalizes on the properties of quantum mechanics. Through the entanglement of particle pairs, information can be encoded into quantum states such that any attempt at eavesdropping would lead to a detectable disturbance in the system. When two parties, say Alice and Bob, wish to communicate securely, they can generate a coherent pair of entangled photons. Each can independently measure their respective photons to create a shared key. Due to the principles of quantum mechanics, if an intruder attempts to intercept or measure the state of the photons, the entanglement is broken, thereby alerting Alice and Bob to the presence of eavesdropping. This revolutionary approach ensures that the very act of eavesdropping can be observed, rendering traditional hacking tactics ineffective.

The applications of this secured communication system stand in stark contrast to classical communication methods, which rely on complex mathematical algorithms to conceal information. While such systems can offer a degree of security, they are ultimately bound by the limitations of classical encryption, which can be compromised through advances in computing power or the emergence of quantum computing. In contrast, the security bestowed by QKD is rooted in the laws of physics themselves, offering a level of protection not dependent on the complexity of algorithms but rather on the fundamental properties of quantum information. This makes it a robust solution against the emerging threat posed by quantum computers capable of breaking classical encryption schemes.

As we consider the future possibilities and innovations in QKD, the potential for scaling this technology into a broader, interconnected quantum communication network becomes apparent. The concept of a "Quantum Internet" is an exciting prospect where secure communication channels exist globally, interconnected through quantum repeaters that maintain entanglement across long distances. The development of such a network would not only heighten security for everyday communications but also enable new forms of digital interaction, potentially transforming how we share information across organizational, governmental, and personal spheres.

Looking ahead, the implications of integrating QKD and other quantum communication technologies into existing infrastructures present a transformational opportunity. As businesses, governments, and individuals increasingly rely on secure communications, the adoption of quantum systems could drive innovations in various fields, including finance, healthcare, and national security. For instance, in finance, quantum-secured communication could protect sensitive transactional data, making financial systems more resilient to hacking attempts. In healthcare, patient privacy could be safeguarded through secure communication channels that ensure confidential data remains protected against unauthorized access.

Yet, as we delve into the landscape of quantum communication and its broader implications, it is essential also to address the ethical considerations that arise from adopting these transformative technologies. The application of QKD raises significant questions regarding privacy and surveillance in an era where information security is paramount. While the promise of enhanced security is enticing, it also necessitates conversations surrounding the potential for misuse or overreach in monitoring communication, demanding a careful balance between implementing protective measures and preserving individual freedoms.

Furthermore, the advent of quantum communication technologies may inadvertently exacerbate existing inequalities. Access to secure communication systems could create divides based on socioeconomic status, technology availability, and education. Therefore, initiatives aimed at ensuring equitable access to quantum-secured communication must be prioritized to prevent further entrenchment of disparities in digital security across different demographics.

In summary, quantum key distribution represents a significant leap forward in securing communications through the lens of quantum mechanics. By offering protections rooted in the fundamental properties of particles, QKD reshapes our understanding of privacy and opens up possibilities for secure communication networks on an unprecedented scale. However, as we navigate the future implications of these technologies, ethical considerations surrounding privacy, equity, and responsible usage must guide the development and deployment of quantum communication systems. As we stand on the brink of this quantum revolution, the landscape of connectivity promises not only innovation but also an opportunity for deeper conversations around the values we place on security, privacy, and equitable access to these extraordinary advancements.

6.3. Securing Communications with Entanglement

Securing communications using quantum entanglement stands at the forefront of the emerging technologies anticipated to arise from the field of quantum mechanics. At its core, this approach represents a fundamental shift in how we perceive and implement security, offering a method of communication that not only carries information but does so with an inherent guarantee of privacy and integrity. This section delves into the mechanisms and implications of leveraging quantum entanglement to secure communications, highlighting its superiority over classical methods and its profound potential to transform our interactions in an increasingly connected world.

To understand how entanglement secures communications, it is essential to grasp the basic principle of quantum states. When two particles become entangled, the state of one particle instantaneously influences the state of the other, even when separated by vast distances. This non-locality creates a unique scenario in which information can be shared without the risk of interception in the traditional sense. Entrenchment in this principle allows the generation of cryptographic keys that are uniquely resistant to unauthorized access.

One of the primary mechanisms to secure communication through entanglement is Quantum Key Distribution (QKD). QKD involves the creation and distribution of cryptographic keys using entangled particles—typically photons. Alice and Bob can generate a shared secret key by encoding information in the states of their respective entangled photons. If an eavesdropper, Eve, attempts to intercept the photons and measure their states, the entanglement is disrupted, revealing her presence. The security of this method rests not on complex algorithms but on the fundamental laws of quantum physics —any interference or measurement collapses the quantum state and alerts the communicating parties to potential security breaches.

This provision of inherently secure communication illustrates a fundamental advantage over classical methods, which rely on mathematical algorithms for encryption that can be broken given sufficient computational power or sophistication. As quantum computing continues to advance, traditional encryption methods are increasingly vulnerable to breaches. Quantum entanglement, in contrast, is impervious to such threats, rendering it a promising solution for secure communications across various sectors, from finance to national security.

In practice, the implementation of quantum-secured communication presents several real-world applications that could reshape entire industries. For instance, in finance, secure transactions over quantum communication channels would effectively eliminate the risk of hacking, as the very act of interception would evoke a detectable disturbance in the quantum signals. Similarly, government communications could employ quantum key distribution to safeguard sensitive information, ensuring that crucial data remains within the hands of authorized individuals only.

Moreover, the integration of entanglement into existing communication technologies offers a pathway for developing a Quantum Internet —a network of quantum communication systems united by entangled particles. This vision entails the deployment of quantum repeaters that maintain the coherence of entangled states over long distances, enhancing the security and efficiency of data transfer. The establishment of such a network promises to revolutionize communication, creating environments where secure data exchange is instantaneous and robust.

However, realizing the full potential of securing communications with quantum entanglement comes with its own set of challenges. One pertinent issue is the fragility of entangled states. When communicating over extended distances, maintaining coherence and mitigating decoherence—interactions with the environment that disrupt quantum states—becomes critical. Researchers are actively developing solutions to preserve entanglement over long distances, working on innovations such as quantum repeaters and error correction protocols to safeguard the integrity of long-distance communications.

Additionally, the need for specialized infrastructure to support quantum communication—the hardware, software, and protocols—represents another hurdle to widespread adoption. Notably, organizations and governments must invest in the development of quantum-compatible systems that allow for seamless integration into existing communication frameworks.

Ethical considerations inevitably arise in deploying technologies that leverage quantum entanglement for secure communication. As societal reliance on secure data transmission amplifies, discussions surrounding the potential for government surveillance and individual privacy must be prioritized. Striking a balance between leveraging advanced technologies for security while ensuring that civil liberties are upheld represents a crucial conversation as we navigate the future landscape of communication.

In summary, securing communications with quantum entanglement embodies a transformative approach to information security, harnessing the laws of quantum mechanics to create robust and unbreakable communication channels. By leveraging mechanisms such as quantum key distribution, this technology offers an unparalleled level of security for critical data transfers across various sectors. As we forge ahead into this quantum-driven future, it is vital to address the challenges and ethical considerations surrounding implementation to ensure that the benefits of these advancements extend equitably to all. The promise of entangled communications not only offers hope for superior security but also challenges our very understanding of privacy and presence in a connected world.

6.4. Comparisons with Classical Communication Methods

In the context of exploring communication technologies, comparing quantum communication methods with classical counterparts reveals a stark contrast that not only highlights the innovations brought forth by quantum mechanics but also underscores the limitations of traditional methods. The roots of classical communication methods lie firmly in the principles of classical physics, primarily relying on electromagnetic waves to transmit information across distances. These methods, while historically effective, are constrained by the laws of physics, ultimately limiting their speed, security, and efficiency.

Classical communication predominantly uses systems like telephones, radio, and standard internet protocols, all of which operate under the premise that signals are transmitted via defined channels subject to degradation and interference. The information is encoded in varying states such as electrical signals or electromagnetic waves, requiring complex infrastructure that often incurs physical limitations. While such systems have advanced steadily over decades, concerns regarding bandwidth limitations, latency issues, and security threats have culminated in the urgent need for innovative solutions.

In stark contrast, quantum communication fundamentally alters the paradigm by introducing the concepts of superposition and entanglement—principles that allow quantum states to express multiple values simultaneously and create non-local connections, respectively. Secure quantum key distribution (QKD) exemplifies how entangled channels enable instantaneous secure communication devoid of interference risks. Where classical systems rely on complex encryption algorithms to secure data, QKD guarantees that any attempt at eavesdropping is fundamentally detectable due to the nature of quantum measurement itself. This intrinsic security mechanism provides a robust safeguard against breaches that classical encryptions cannot compete with.

While classical communication methods create vulnerabilities, particularly as cybersecurity threats evolve, quantum communication offers a paradigm shift that presents both an opportunity and a necessity for future-proofing the methods by which we share information. In practical terms, this means that secure channels established through quantum mechanics could eliminate the specter of hacking as the disruptive effects of intrusion would manifest practically—thus rendering quantum-secured communications essential for industries reliant on sensitive data.

Another critical point of comparison is the speed and efficiency of information transfer. Classical communication is intrinsically limited by the speed of light and can be subject to delays caused by physical barriers, network congestion, or technological constraints. Even with improvements in fiber optics and satellite communication, latency remains a critical problem, particularly in real-time applications. Quantum communication, leveraging entangled particles, holds the potential for instantaneous data exchange, thereby facilitating real-time communication without the delays typically encountered in classical systems. This innovation encapsulates the essence of enhancing telepresence, where users can interact as if co-located —fostering richer, more authentic connections that transcend traditional interactions.

Exploring the potential for integration with existing communication systems raises the question of how next-generation quantum communication technologies will coexist with established infrastructures. While classical systems dominate today's communication landscape, the integration of quantum technologies presents a unique challenge that necessitates novel paradigms for data exchange. Hybrid systems may emerge, where quantum principles can augment classical methods, paving the way for quantum-classical networks that maximize both security and usability.

As organizations and sectors begin to adopt quantum communication methods, they must also confront challenges, particularly concerning infrastructure and scalability. Classical systems require extensive resources, and transitioning to quantum-compatible frameworks demands significant investment and a reimagining of existing workflows. Developing scalable quantum communication networks strengthens the case for practicality—this will require extensive research, development, and field trials to ensure that quantum technologies can be reliably deployed on an organizational scale.

Moreover, ethical concerns surrounding quantum communication emphasize the profound implications of such technologies on privacy, consent, and surveillance. A transition to quantum-secured communications raises critical questions about who controls access to these technologies, how they are implemented, and what regulatory frameworks need to be established to protect individual rights and freedoms. Ensuring equitable access to quantum communication technology becomes vital as the benefits could otherwise exacerbate existing inequalities.

Additionally, the rapid evolution of quantum communication methods may alter the social dynamics of how we communicate and interact. Enhanced real-time communication could lead to significant transformations in workplace cultures and interpersonal relationships, fostering deeper connections but also prompting concerns about the potential for overreach or technology-induced pressures.

In summary, the comparison between quantum communication methods and classical communication reveals a transformative shift that challenges our preconceptions regarding data transfer, security, and interaction. Quantum communication leverages the principles of quantum mechanics to eradicate vulnerabilities present in classical systems while facilitating real-time interactions that deepen connections among individuals. As we progress toward greater integration of quantum technologies, it is essential to remain cognizant of the implications these advancements hold for society and the ethical considerations they invoke. The future of communication is poised for a revolutionary shift, where the transformative potential of quantum principles paves new pathways for connectivity, security, and human experience.

6.5. Future Possibilities and Innovations

Envisioning the Future of Quantum Proxy is a journey into the possibilities that unfold when quantum mechanics and cutting-edge technology converge to reshape our understanding of communication. As we stand at the crossroads of a new technological era, the prospect of Quantum Proxy opens doors to transformative innovations that promise to redefine human interactions, presence, and connection in profound ways.

At its essence, Quantum Proxy encompasses the application of quantum entanglement and superposition to create seamless telepresence experiences. As we look to the future, we can imagine a world where geographical barriers dissipate, allowing individuals to connect and share experiences as if they were physically together. This redefinition of what it means to be "present" may lead to a paradigm shift in remote communication, enabling real-time exchanges that are rich, immersive, and intimate.

The journey from concept to reality involves several critical steps. First, it is vital to focus on the development of robust quantum communication networks capable of ensuring secure, instantaneous connections. Current advancements in quantum key distribution (QKD) exemplify the foundational work underway to create systems that leverage entangled states for enhanced security. These networks will serve as the backbone of Quantum Proxy technology, facilitating instantaneous data transfer and interaction without the vulnerabilities that plague classical systems.

The path to quantum ubiquity also hinges on interdisciplinary collaboration. The integration of quantum principles across various sectors necessitates partnerships among physicists, engineers, technologists, and sociologists. These collaborations must address the multifaceted challenges of implementing Quantum Proxy, including the scaling of technology, ensuring security, and developing user-friendly interfaces that make quantum communication accessible to the general population. Holding regular workshops, seminars, and forums can foster dialogue among stakeholders, sharing insights and aligning goals for a common vision of the future.

As we envision future innovations in Quantum Proxy, we must consider its impact across diverse fields. In healthcare, telepresence facilitated by quantum technology could revolutionize patient care by enabling real-time consultations between healthcare professionals and patients, transcending geographical barriers and delivering expert opinions when needed most. Moreover, medical training could see advancements through immersive simulations that leverage quantum-enhanced telepresence, allowing medical students to learn and practice alongside seasoned professionals in a highly interactive environment.

In education, Quantum Proxy has the potential to create global classrooms where students from various backgrounds interact, collaborate, and share knowledge in real-time. By harnessing quantum entanglement, educators can facilitate experiences where students feel a profound sense of connection to both their peers and the subject matter, creating a richer learning environment that fosters engagement and curiosity.

The implications for the entertainment industry are equally exciting. Imagine virtual reality experiences where participants can attend concerts, theater performances, or immersive storytelling events as if they were present. The authenticity of shared experiences through Quantum Proxy could redefine the entertainment landscape, facilitating interactions that are not merely observational but participatory and emotional.

As we delve deeper into envisioning the future of Quantum Proxy, considerations around ethics and equity must be addressed. Any advancement in quantum technology should prioritize inclusivity, ensuring access across demographics to avoid exacerbating existing inequalities. Ethical frameworks should guide the development and implementation of Quantum Proxy, promoting responsible usage of technology that respects individual rights, privacy, and personal agency.

Looking ahead, the question remains: how can we reconcile the aspirations of innovative technology with the moral responsibilities that come with it? As we navigate the uncharted waters of quantum communications, prioritizing ethical considerations and engaging stakeholders in open dialogues can help forge paths that balance progress with accountability.

The global effects of Quantum Proxy promise a transformative impact on how we engage with one another and interpret presence. Envision a future where distance becomes a relative concept in human interactions—where sharing experiences is immediate and authentic. The collective potential of Quantum Proxy across sectors encourages us to dream bigger, innovate further, and deepen connections—all while holding steadfast to the ethical and moral responsibility that accompanies such extraordinary capabilities.

In conclusion, envisioning the future of Quantum Proxy invites us to reimagine communication, interaction, and presence. As quantum mechanics permeates our realities, we embark on a journey characterized not only by technological advancement but also by the promise of enriched human experiences. This transformative potential beckons us to actively shape a world integrated with quantum possibilities, heralding an era where the boundaries of connection are expanded and redefined, ultimately bridging gaps between individuals in an increasingly interconnected existence. The future of Quantum Proxy is not merely a technological innovation; it stands as a testament to human ingenuity, creativity, and an enduring commitment to deepening the bonds that unite us.

7. Ethics and Implications of Quantum Proxy

7.1. Ethical Considerations in Emerging Technology

In the exploration of emerging technologies such as Quantum Proxy, ethical considerations play a pivotal role in shaping our understanding and acceptance of these advancements. Ethics in technology is not merely an ancillary discussion but a fundamental necessity that informs the development, deployment, and societal integration of transformative innovations. As quantum technologies advance, particularly in the realm of telepresence and communication, we must critically examine the ethical implications and responsibilities entailed in their applications.

The rapid pace of technological advancements often outstrips our established ethical frameworks, leading to complex dilemmas. One of the primary concerns surrounding emerging technologies is the potential for misuse, manipulation, and unintended consequences that arise from their implementation. Quantum Proxy, with its promise of instantaneous communication and deeper connections, raises several ethical questions related to consent, privacy, and the authenticity of experiences. The ability to be "present" in multiple locations simultaneously could blur the lines of reality, complicating our understanding of interpersonal relationships and individual identity.

Furthermore, the implications of quantum communication technologies on privacy are profound. As quantum key distribution offers unprecedented security in data transmission, it also poses challenges regarding surveillance and individual freedoms. The ability to share experiences instantly could entice unauthorized surveillance practices under the guise of enhanced security. Thus, the implications of privacy protection become paramount as we consider the deployment of technologies capable of reshaping the very fabric of human interaction.

Equally important are the social dynamics that emerging technologies can influence. Quantum Proxy has the potential to democratize communication, breaking down geographical barriers and facilitating global interactions. However, this ushering in of new possibilities could also exacerbate existing inequalities if access to these technologies is not equitable. Disparities in technology adoption and infrastructure can create divides amongst different socio-economic groups, leading to a future where only a subset of individuals fully benefits from quantum advancements.

Additionally, addressing moral and legal challenges is critical in the context of Quantum Proxy. As we incorporate quantum technologies, we must grapple with the moral responsibilities that arise from their use. For instance, if telepresence becomes a ubiquitous aspect of daily life, how do we navigate cases of consent, especially when interactions transcend physical boundaries? Robust frameworks must be established to ensure that ethical considerations are prioritized during the development stages, allowing us to navigate the complexities introduced by these capabilities.

Balancing advancement with responsibility is crucial. As societies embrace quantum technologies, stakeholders must engage in proactive discussions that address ethical considerations rather than react passively to challenges as they arise. Establishing guidelines and regulatory measures that govern the use of Quantum Proxy will be essential to protect individual rights and foster a climate of trust. Encouraging transparency, accountability, and community engagement in technological development can help mitigate risks and foster equitable access and use.

Moreover, fostering ethical technology development requires integrating diverse perspectives. Initiatives involving ethicists, community leaders, technologists, and policymakers can provide a holistic view of the implications inherent in emerging technologies. Such multidisciplinary collaboration can inform the ethical conversations surrounding the deployment of quantum technologies, ensuring that they align with societal values and expectations.

In conclusion, ethical considerations in emerging technologies such as Quantum Proxy represent a critical area for exploration. As the potential for transformative communication unfolds through quantum mechanics, it is essential to critically engage with the implications of these advancements. Addressing concerns regarding privacy, equity, and moral responsibilities allows us to navigate the complexities associated with Quantum Proxy technologies responsibly. By prioritizing ethical dialogues and collaborative efforts, we can ensure that the evolution of quantum technologies fosters an inclusive and equitable future where the benefits extend to all individuals in society. The journey ahead beckons us to balance innovation with our collective responsibility to uphold ethical standards, guiding us toward a future where technology serves as a force for good.

7.2. Impact on Privacy and Surveillance

The impact of quantum technologies, particularly in the context of Quantum Proxy, represents a significant shift in how we conceptualize privacy and surveillance. In a world increasingly influenced by the digital landscape, the ability to communicate and share experiences in real-time through quantum entanglement opens up a complex set of ethical and practical considerations regarding the management of information, interactions, and personal data.

Central to this discussion is the concept of privacy, which is fundamentally redefined by the capabilities of Quantum Proxy. In traditional communication systems, privacy is managed through encryption and security protocols that aim to protect data from unauthorized access. However, quantum communication takes this to an entirely new level by offering built-in security mechanisms through Quantum Key Distribution (QKD). This method utilizes the principles of quantum mechanics to ensure that any attempt to eavesdrop on a communication channel is detectable. The inherent security derived from quantum principles creates a compelling case for enhanced privacy. It is important, however, to remember that while quantum technologies can bolster security, they can also facilitate new forms of surveillance that need to be carefully monitored.

For instance, the very nature of telepresence enabled by Quantum Proxy may lead to environments where surveillance mechanisms can be seamlessly integrated into communication systems. The potential for users to be constantly accessible and monitored raises questions about the boundaries of surveillance and consent. It calls into question the ethical implications of how these technologies could be employed—whether by individuals, corporations, or governments. The challenge lies in establishing robust ethical frameworks to safeguard against potential abuses, ensuring that the benefits of quantum communication do not come at the cost of individual freedoms and privacy rights.

Moreover, the manner in which data is shared and communicated in a quantum context may have implications for societal norms surrounding privacy. As Quantum Proxy technology creates new avenues for connection and communication, the expectation of privacy may shift. With the ability to transmit personal experiences and interactions instantaneously, individuals may unconsciously adopt more transparent interactions, thereby redefining what privacy means in the digital age. This evolution necessitates a reevaluation of individual and collective boundaries concerning privacy and consent.

Another aspect of the impact of Quantum Proxy on privacy and surveillance concerns the potential for data ownership and control. In a world where telepresence and communication could potentially become ubiquitous, determining who owns the data generated during these interactions becomes critical. The ethical considerations surrounding personal data ownership, consent, and privacy rights will need to be addressed as Quantum Proxy technologies develop. Engaging in discussions about data governance frameworks will be essential for establishing ethical guidelines that respect individual autonomy while promoting systemic accountability.

On the other hand, surveillance may evolve to be more sophisticated with the integration of quantum technologies. The very attributes that endow quantum communication with unprecedented security could also be misused by entities seeking to monitor individuals covertly. As quantum algorithms evolve, they may enable data collection methods that are difficult to detect, creating new concerns over covert surveillance tactics. Striking a balance between the protective measures quantum technologies afford against hacking and the potential for misuse through enhanced surveillance capabilities will create a challenging landscape that requires vigilance and proactive governance.

Socioeconomic disparities further complicate the implications of quantum technologies on privacy and surveillance. As quantum advancements usher in superior methods of communication, access to these technologies may become stratified along economic lines, heightening existing inequalities. If only certain segments of society can utilize the benefits of quantum-secured communications, the disparities could lead to unequal privacy protections. Therefore, addressing equity concerns is paramount to ensuring that quantum advancements serve all societal segments, rather than exacerbating divides.

In summary, the impact of Quantum Proxy on privacy and surveillance encompasses a complex interplay of enhanced security, ethical dilemmas, evolving social norms, and socioeconomic considerations. While quantum technologies have the potential to strengthen privacy protections, the concurrent risks associated with their misuse necessitate careful deliberation and responsive governance. The future of privacy in a quantum world will depend on establishing ethical frameworks that not only celebrate technological advancement but also advocate for individual rights and freedoms. As society navigates this new frontier, fostering discussions around the implications of quantum communication will be crucial in shaping a future that values privacy, consent, and equity in an era defined by interconnectivity.

7.3. Social Dynamics and Equity Concerns

In the discourse surrounding Quantum Proxy, particularly in the context of communication technologies, the subchapter on social dynamics and equity concerns emerges as a critical examination of how emerging technologies can reshape interpersonal interactions, societal structures, and overall accessibility. As the capability for instantaneous telepresence through quantum entanglement offers unprecedented potential for human connection, it also prompts vital questions regarding social equity, inclusion, and the disparities that may arise when advanced technologies intersect with everyday life.

The transformative power of Quantum Proxy lies in its promise to bridge distances, thereby redefining physical presence and interaction. Individuals could feasibly share experiences in real-time from disparate geographic locations, enhancing relational dynamics in both personal and professional spheres. For instance, families separated by oceans could engage in shared moments of celebration, while teams across the world could collaborate on projects as if seated together in the same room. This shift has the potential to foster deeper feelings of connection and community, erasing the limitations that distance imposes on relationships.

However, as we embrace this potentially seamless connectivity, we must also critically assess how such advancements may inadvertently perpetuate existing social inequalities. Access to quantum technologies is likely to be influenced by a host of factors, including socioeconomic status, educational background, and infrastructure availability. If Quantum Proxy technology develops in environments where access is limited to affluent communities or organizations, we could see a widening gap between those who benefit from enhanced communication capabilities and those who do not. This disparity could lead to a society where the benefits of quantum advancements are unequally distributed, reinforcing systemic inequalities rather than alleviating them.

Equity concerns extend beyond mere access to technology; they also encompass the way individuals interact with these systems. As Quantum Proxy allows for more profound emotional and experiential sharing, issues surrounding representation and voice become increasingly salient. Who defines the norms of these new telepresence interactions? Will the mainstream use of Quantum Proxy privilege certain communication styles, cultural nuances, or social frameworks over others? Addressing these questions becomes essential to ensure that diverse perspectives are validated within the emerging landscape, promoting inclusivity rather than exclusivity in the virtual environments facilitated by quantum technologies.

Moreover, the social dynamics of adopting Quantum Proxy technologies may evoke shifts in interpersonal relationships and communal structures. With enhanced connectivity, traditional notions of community could evolve, with interactions increasingly occurring in virtual settings rather than physical spaces. While this presents opportunities for global gatherings and cross-cultural exchanges, it also raises concerns about the potential erosion of local communities and the valuable social networks that thrive on physical presence. As individuals navigate relationships predominantly through virtual means, we may need to rediscover and redefine the essence of physical interactions, social bonds, and collective identity.

Educational equity emerges as another critical consideration in the context of Quantum Proxy. Quantum communication technologies hold enormous promise for enriching learning experiences by enabling access to expert knowledge across the globe. However, it is vital to ensure that educational systems and institutions do not further entrench existing inequalities. If schools or communities lack access to the infrastructure required for quantum-enabled learning, students from disadvantaged backgrounds might miss out on pivotal opportunities for growth and development. As such, there is an urgent need to develop initiatives aimed at equipping underserved areas with the necessary tools and resources for engaging with quantum technologies.

Furthermore, the ethical dimensions associated with these advanced technologies necessitate active engagement. As stakeholders advance in developing Quantum Proxy, accompanying discussions regarding data privacy, consent, and surveillance become essential. Just as the capabilities of quantum communication have the potential to enhance security and privacy, they can also introduce risks that demand careful consideration and governance. Striking a balance between harnessing the benefits of Quantum Proxy while ensuring individual rights and protections underscores the importance of ongoing dialogue and regulatory frameworks.

In summary, the discussions around social dynamics and equity concerns in the context of Quantum Proxy highlight the importance of considering the broader implications of emergent technologies. While the potential for enriched human connection and new relational possibilities is palpable, balancing this progress with equity, representation, and ethics is paramount. As we advance into a future that embraces quantum communication technologies, ensuring that these innovations are accessible to all and grounded in the principles of inclusivity, diversity, and fairness will ultimately determine their lasting impact on society. Embracing the promise of Quantum Proxy requires a holistic approach that recognizes the intertwined nature of technology, community, and ethical responsibility, paving the way for a more equitable and connected world.

7.4. Addressing Moral and Legal Challenges

Addressing the moral and legal challenges surrounding the burgeoning technology of Quantum Proxy demands a comprehensive examination of the intersection between advanced quantum capabilities and the ethical frameworks that govern our societies. As the promise of instant telepresence through quantum entanglement emerges, so too do the complexities of its implications for personal freedoms, legal norms, and societal values.

At the forefront of these challenges lies the question of consent. As Quantum Proxy facilitates more profound interactions, the necessity of securing informed consent becomes paramount. Individuals must be aware not only of the nature of their interactions but also of how their data may be utilized, stored, or perhaps redirected in quantum communication environments. The instantaneous nature of quantum entanglement raises the specter of unauthorized surveillance or unintended sharing of experiences. It is essential that both users and developers approach the implementation of Quantum Proxy with a commitment to establishing clear protocols and guidelines that prioritize ethical consent practices.

Additionally, concerning personal data management, the implications of Quantum Proxy will dramatically alter the landscape of data privacy. Traditional frameworks based on classical cryptography must evolve to accommodate the complexities of quantum communications. While quantum key distribution offers heightened security, the integration of quantum technologies necessitates a careful evaluation of data ownership, control, and the permanence of shared experiences. As quantum capabilities allow for real-time, immersive experiences, the ease with which personal information can be collected and analyzed will challenge existing legal frameworks, bringing into question how privacy rights are defined and protected.

Legal jurisdictions will also grapple with the challenges of regulating quantum technologies. Given that Quantum Proxy transcends geographical boundaries in its applications, developing cohesive international legal standards will require collaboration among nations and regulatory bodies. Questions of jurisdiction arise: who is accountable if misuse occurs? How do we address the potential for espionage or cyber warfare using quantum communication systems? Establishing clear guidelines will be vital to ensuring that the advantages of quantum technologies are harnessed responsibly while mitigating risks associated with their misuse.

In grappling with the moralities surrounding Quantum Proxy, we must also navigate the implications of equity and access. The deployment of such transformative technologies could exacerbate existing socio-economic divides. Consider the potential for privileged access to quantum-secured communication channels reserved for affluent organizations or governments while sidelining marginalized communities lacking the resources to engage with advanced technologies. Thus, the moral responsibility to uphold equity becomes critical; as we forge ahead with Quantum Proxy, there must be concerted efforts to democratize access, ensuring that diverse populations are not left behind in the quantum revolution.

Furthermore, as Quantum Proxy evolves, we must consider the broader societal changes it facilitates. The ability to share experiences instantaneously has the potential to shape cultural dynamics, redefine interpersonal relationships, and even alter notions of identity. The advent of hyper-connection through quantum telepresence invites us to reconsider what it means to be present and engaged. Will this shift foster genuine relationships grounded in authenticity, or will it cultivate superficial connections based on the immediacy of shared experiences? Establishing ethical frameworks to guide behaviors in such interconnected environments is imperative to nurture meaning-ful interactions.

A profound transformation in social structures entails a prerequisite dialogue on the ethical implications that will emerge. Researchers, technologists, ethicists, and community leaders must collectively engage in discussions that unpack the ethical responsibilities of devel-oping and deploying Quantum Proxy technologies. These dialogues need to emphasize the importance of user agency, transparency, and accountability in all phases of technology implementation.

Moreover, establishing an adaptive regulatory framework that evolves alongside technological advancements is crucial. Policymak-ers must engage with experts to understand the nuances of quantum capabilities, fostering laws and regulations reflective of both current realities and future projections. Companies developing quantum technologies should also be held accountable to ethical standards that prioritize user dignity and respect.

In conclusion, the moral and legal challenges posed by Quantum Proxy demand a vigorous, proactive approach to ensure its ethical implementation. Upholding principles of consent, privacy, equity, and responsible innovation will be fundamental as we navigate the realms where quantum technologies intersect with human experiences. Con-tinued dialogue and collaboration among stakeholders will be vital to guide the responsible development of Quantum Proxy, ensuring that the tapestry of connections it weaves serves humanity as a transfor-mative force—one that amplifies the inherent value of relationships rather than diminishes them. As we tread this path, it is our collective responsibility to ensure that the promise of instant telepresence is realized in ways that honor the principles of dignity, respect, and equity across the human experience.

7.5. Balancing Advancement and Responsibility

In an era marked by rapid technological advancements, the concept of Quantum Proxy invites significant exploration into the realms of ethical responsibility. The integration of quantum technologies into communication has ushered in profound opportunities for transformation; however, it also necessitates careful consideration of the moral implications that accompany such innovations. As we navigate the delicate balance between leveraging the immense potential of quantum entanglement for instant telepresence and ensuring responsibility toward societal norms and ethical standards, we find ourselves at a pivotal intersection.

The promise of Quantum Proxy to redefine communication through instantaneous interactions offers unparalleled opportunities for connection, collaboration, and innovation. Yet, this technological evolution also prompts critical reflections on the ethical use of such capabilities. At the forefront lies the notion of consent: with the ability to share experiences in real-time, the question of whether individuals fully understand and agree to how their data and interactions are being utilized becomes paramount. As Quantum Proxy blurs the lines between physical presence and virtual interactions, users must possess awareness of their agency and control over personal data in these quantum-enabled environments.

Moreover, privacy presents another layer of ethical complexity in the age of Quantum Proxy. While quantum key distribution provides enhanced security measures to safeguard data transmission, the interconnectivity afforded by this technology could also facilitate intrusive surveillance mechanisms, both by state and non-state actors. The concern here is twofold: while individuals may gain access to secure communication channels, the capacity for constant monitoring could lead to a society where privacy is diminished, and surveillance becomes normalized under the guise of security. Establishing rigorous guidelines and frameworks will be essential to navigate the tensions between security and individual privacy, ensuring that the benefits of technology do not come at a prohibitive cost to personal freedoms.

Equity and access to Quantum Proxy also warrant careful ethical consideration. As quantum communication technologies continue to evolve, the risk arises that they could further entrench existing disparities in technology access. If implementation remains confined to well-resourced institutions or economically advantaged populations, we could witness a widening gap between those who reap the advantages of quantum advancements and those left behind. As we envision a future shaped by Quantum Proxy, promoting equitable access to quantum technologies across demographics will be essential. This commitment necessitates cultivating platforms for dialogue and collaboration aimed at democratizing technology and ensuring that marginalized communities are included in the quantum revolution.

While the advancements heralded by Quantum Proxy promise transformative experiences, they also generate moral dilemmas regarding human relationships and societal norms. The ability to engage remotely through quantum-enabled interactions presents opportunities for deeper connection, yet it raises concerns about the authenticity of interactions cultivated in a virtual environment. As connections facilitated by Quantum Proxy flourish, individuals may grapple with questions of presence, identity, and the essence of relationships. Balancing the potential for heightened connectivity with the risks of superficial engagement will be crucial as society adapts to new paradigms of communication.

As we anticipate the ethical challenges that Quantum Proxy technologies may invoke, we must also prioritize a culture of active engagement among stakeholders. Ensuring that developers, researchers, policymakers, and communities converse and collaborate reinforces collective responsibility toward ethical development. By creating interdisciplinary networks centered around technology, ethics, and social impacts, we can nurture an ecosystem that not only encourages innovation but also imposes accountability in the deployment of these transformative technologies.

In conclusion, as we plunge deeper into the possibilities of Quantum Proxy and its implications for communication technologies, the importance of balancing advancement with ethical responsibility cannot be overstated. The journey ahead must prioritize considerations of consent, privacy, equity, and the evolving nature of human relationships. By fostering inclusive discussions and addressing ethical complexities, we can pave the way toward realizing the promise of Quantum Proxy as a catalyst for enhanced human connection, ensuring that its benefits resonate equitably across society. The interplay between quantum innovation and ethical responsibility will define the trajectory of this technology as we navigate the uncharted waters of an increasingly interconnected future. Embracing this duality with intention and vigilance is our path forward, shaping a world where technology uplifts the human experience rather than diminishing it.

8. Quantum Proxy in Communication Technologies

8.1. Enhancing Communication Networks

In the quest to enhance communication networks through Quantum Proxy, we delve into how the integration of quantum mechanics fundamentally transforms traditional interaction paradigms. The revolutionary potential of quantum entanglement and superposition paves the way for novel applications that redefine communication across various sectors. By harnessing quantum states, the communication landscape can be reshaped, promising improved efficiency, security, and immediacy in human connection.

The essence of enhancing communication networks through quantum technology lies in the immediate capabilities afforded by entanglement and superposition. Standard classical communication systems—whether via telephone, email, or video conferencing—are bound by physical limitations. The speed of light imposes constraints on how quickly information can be transmitted, while also exposing channels to risk of interception and hacking. Quantum Proxy, conversely, bypasses these limitations by enabling instantaneous data exchange that is inherently secure.

One of the most significant advancements lies in the creation of quantum communication networks that utilize entangled particles for data transmission. These networks leverage quantum key distribution (QKD) to ensure secure communication channels are maintained. Through established protocols, quantum entanglement allows for secure generation of cryptographic keys between users, providing privacy assurance that is unprecedented in traditional methods. As users connect via these quantum networks, their interactions can occur in real-time without the fear of eavesdropping or data breaches, thereby fostering deeper trust in communication systems.

As we envision practical implementations, enhancing communication networks through Quantum Proxy also entails opportunities for real-time remote interactions. Consider a scenario where family members geographically separated by vast distances can share moments of joy —birthdays, weddings, or reunions—through immersive telepresence facilitated by quantum technology. Using the properties of quantum entanglement, users may feel as if they are in the same room, sharing experiences with emotional resonance akin to physical proximity. Such innovation promises to bridge gaps in connection, enhancing relationships and enabling meaningful interactions that transcend geographical constraints.

The realm of virtual meetings and conferences stands to be profoundly transformed as well. Organizations can leverage quantum-enhanced communication networks to conduct meetings that allow participants from across continents to engage collaboratively in real-time while feeling deeply connected. Imagine a board meeting where every participant, despite being miles apart, shares the same virtual space with instantaneous audio and visual feedback. Quantum Proxy ensures seamless interaction by eliminating latency, allowing spontaneous exchanges of ideas that lead to more dynamic and effective discussions.

In sectors like media and entertainment, the impact of quantum communication is equally transformative. Audiences may participate in live performances or immersive experiences, projecting themselves into shared virtual environments through quantum proxies. The ability to feel connected to live events—be it concerts, theater productions, or film screenings—could redefine how individuals consume and engage with media. This paradigm shift opens the door to collaborative storytelling where creators and audiences alike can interact fluidly, enriching the narrative experience and establishing deeper relational connections.

The landscape of research surrounding quantum communication is expanding. Breakthroughs in quantum communication technologies have led to innovative applications that bridge theoretical concepts with real-world challenges. International collaborations among research institutions have fostered the development of pilot quantum networks, where entangled particles secure communications over vast distances. As we observe these advances, we gain insights into the feasibility and scalability of quantum-enhanced communication networks that promise to transform societal interaction.

Thus, the journey of enhancing communication networks through Quantum Proxy provides us the opportunity to rethink our traditional notions of connection, presence, and interaction. The embrace of quantum mechanics heralds an era where instant communication becomes the norm, allowing for richer, more authentic shared experiences regardless of distance. As we navigate this transformative frontier, an equitable approach to integration ensures that the benefits of quantum communication flow widely, ensuring a connected global society that cherishes the power of presence in an ever-evolving technological landscape. The integration of Quantum Proxy marks the dawn of a new epoch where communication is liberated from constraints, allowing humanity to flourish through interconnectedness and authentic relationships across the globe.

8.2. Remote Interactions in Real-Time

Remote interactions in real-time have become an exhilarating focal point as we explore the revolutionary implications of Quantum Proxy technology within the realm of communication. The ability to engage with one another across vast physical divides, as if sharing the same space, challenges our conventional understanding of presence and connection. Utilizing the principles of quantum entanglement, which allow for instantaneous information sharing regardless of distance, we can reimagine how we connect personally, collaboratively, and societally in a world transformed by quantum mechanics.

At the core of remote interactions enhanced by Quantum Proxy lies the principle of entanglement, which permits a pair of particles to remain in consistent correlation, such that the state of one can have immediate effects on the state of the other, no matter how far apart they are. This characteristic enables the seamless transmission of data that fundamentally alters the parameters of traditional remote communication. With this ability to share experiences instantaneously, the potential for Quantum Proxy to elevate human interactions is vast and varied.

Real-time remote interactions promise to transcend the limitations imposed by current video conferencing and communication technologies. Traditional methods are often marred by latency, bandwidth constraints, and the lack of sensory engagement, resulting in interactions that may feel flat or disconnected. With quantum-enhanced telepresence, however, individuals might encounter sensations that transcend mere visual and auditory inputs. Imagine a world where a loved one's laughter resonates with contextual depth, where physical gestures are perceptible, and where the emotional nuances of conversations are palpable. The ability to experience a sense of presence, regardless of geographical barriers, could redefine personal relationships, enabling individuals to maintain closer bonds despite physical separation.

The implications of such advancements extend into professional domains as well. In a landscape where remote work is becoming increasingly common, Quantum Proxy technology promises a new paradigm for collaborative interactions. Virtual meetings would evolve into immersive experiences with participants feeling as if they are physically present in the same room. Teams distributed across continents could engage in brainstorming sessions, share ideas, and provide instantaneous feedback without the traditional latency that disrupts the flow of conversation in standard video conferences. Such capabilities empower organizations to operate with enhanced agility and creativity, leveraging talent from around the world while fostering authentic collaborations.

Educational environments stand to gain considerable enhancement through the integration of Quantum Proxy as well. Classroom experiences could transition from physically fixed spaces to virtual learning environments where students engage with teachers and peers actively. Imagine attending a conference with leading experts in real-time discussions, participating in experiential learning, collaborating on projects, and activating a collective intellectual curiosity.

The potential here is not just limited to knowledge dissemination but also to the cultivation of a global community of learners who engage in meaningful ways, challenging traditional educational models.

Furthermore, the cultural and entertainment sectors could undergo significant shifts. Quantum Proxy technology enables audiences from different parts of the world to partake in live events together, experiencing music concerts or theatrical performances as if they were physically present. As audiences share these moments in real-time, the emotional resonance deepens, thereby enhancing the communal aspects of art and culture. The canvas of creativity expands as storytelling becomes interactive—viewers could shift narratives through remote engagements, influencing the direction of a story or a performance.

While the promise of real-time remote interactions through Quantum Proxy is profoundly transformative, it is equally essential to address the accompanying challenges. The journey towards realizing these advancements necessitates overcoming technological barriers, such as maintaining coherence in quantum states, addressing infrastructure limitations, and ensuring robust error-correction protocols that preserve the integrity of quantum communications. Ethical considerations, including issues of privacy and consent surrounding personal data sharing in virtual environments, must also remain at the forefront of discussions.

In conclusion, the potential for enhancing remote interactions in real-time through Quantum Proxy technology paves the way for a revolutionary shift in how we communicate and connect. By leveraging the principles of quantum entanglement, we can transcend traditional limitations and engage in richer, more authentic experiences that redefine personal relationships, collaboration, education, and cultural sharing. As we navigate the complexities of implementing such transformative technologies, it is crucial to prioritize ethical frameworks and collaborative efforts to ensure that the benefits of Quantum Proxy are accessible and equitable, unlocking a future characterized by interconnectedness and profound human experiences. The essence of engaging with others, irrespective of physical distance, holds the promise of an evolving reality where presence is not confined by location, but is boundless and immersive, enriching the tapestry of human connection.

8.3. Virtual Meetings and Conferences

In recent years, the landscape of communication technology has been transformed by the proliferation of virtual meetings and conferences, particularly driven by the need for remote interactions. As the world increasingly embraces digital platforms for professional engagement, the potential for Quantum Proxy, a revolutionary concept harnessing the principles of quantum mechanics, emerges as a game-changer in reimagining these virtual experiences.

The reality of virtual meetings as we know them today is shaped by widespread adoption driven by factors such as globalization, remote work, and the efficiencies offered by digital communication. Traditional platforms, however, often grapple with limitations, including latency, noise, and the absence of genuine presence—attributes that can hinder collaborative efforts and diminish emotional engagement. Quantum Proxy technology offers the tantalizing possibility of solving these issues, creating a means of engaging remotely that feels remarkably authentic and seamless.

At its core, Quantum Proxy leverages quantum entanglement and superposition principles to facilitate instantaneous information transfer. Imagine a virtual meeting where participants, regardless of their geographical locations, feel as if they are in the same room— where audio and visual input are truly synchronized in real time. The approach can dissolve the physical distance and technological delays characteristic of classical communication methods, enabling discussions that flow naturally, devoid of the lags that typically disrupt conversations in virtual settings.

Quantum Proxy can redefine the interactive dynamic within virtual meetings. Utilizing entangled particles, participants may share information and experiences instantaneously, an enhancement made possible by quantum communication. The prospect of engaging in discussions with colleagues where non-verbal cues, emotional resonances, and spontaneous reactions are perceptible transforms the nature of collaboration. This experience promises to enhance creativity, foster innovation, and deepen interpersonal connections, vital elements that are often diminished in conventional virtual meetings.

Further, the application of Quantum Proxy in conferences opens new avenues for immersive experiences. Imagine attending a global conference where experts and thought leaders share insights, and attendees can participate interactively, asking questions and contributing opinions just as they would in a physical audience. The potential for quantum-enhanced telepresence could lead to a richer exchange of ideas where diversity of thought flourishes through seamless dialogue.

Moreover, the potential for these advancements extends beyond mere participation in formal meetings. Social interactions often occur at conferences, such as networking breaks or informal discussions. Quantum Proxy provides opportunities for virtual spaces that mimic these social interactions, allowing attendees to engage with one another freely and authentically. Consider the ramifications of this technology for industry gatherings, education symposiums, and cultural exhibitions where participation can take on new dimensions, cultivating a sense of community that transcends physical spaces.

As organizations recognize the advantages of incorporating Quantum Proxy technology, the implications for business communications are likely to be profound. High-stakes negotiations, crucial decision-making processes, and even training sessions could all benefit from quantum-enhanced connection, ultimately leading to improved outcomes and greater organizational agility. Empowered by real-time interactions that draw on the emotional resonance and nuance that define human engagement, businesses may discover new pathways toward fostering teamwork, inclusivity, and resilience in an evolving landscape.

Despite the immense promise, embracing Quantum Proxy in virtual meetings and conferences comes with a set of challenges that must be addressed. Establishing robust quantum communication networks requires significant investments in infrastructural development, including the creation of quantum repeaters to maintain entanglement over distances. Moreover, the ethical implications of such technology must be evaluated diligently, particularly regarding privacy, consent, and equitable access as quantum communication systems become integrated within organizational frameworks.

As we look ahead, the impact of Quantum Proxy on virtual meetings and conferences holds transformative potential, paving the way for a new realm of remote interactions characterized by authenticity, presence, and engagement. By embracing this technology, organizations can redefine their communication strategies, creating an environment where collaboration knows no boundaries. The prospect of quantum-enhanced telepresence invites us to dream bigger and push the limits of what it means to connect in an increasingly interconnected world. In doing so, we will unlock opportunities that extend far beyond the boundaries of our current understanding, paving the way for a communication landscape enriched by the extraordinary capabilities of quantum mechanics.

8.4. Impacts on Media and Entertainment

The emergence of quantum technologies not only promises to revolutionize the fabric of communication but also has profound implications for the media and entertainment industries. As we delve into the impacts of these technologies on media and entertainment, the potential for Quantum Proxy—enabled by quantum entanglement—offers novel avenues for interaction, engagement, and creativity that extend far beyond the constraints of classical methods.

At the heart of this transformation is the ability of quantum communication to facilitate real-time connections that defy conventional limitations. Traditional media platforms often grapple with the inherent latency of digital communication—a barrier that can diminish the immediacy and connectivity of shared experiences. Quantum

Proxy, however, promises a future where distance becomes inconsequential, allowing audiences to engage in live events, performances, and collaborative storytelling with a compelling sense of presence. This redefinition of presence invites a broader understanding of how individuals—whether artists, audiences, or participants—interact with media.

Consider the possibilities for live performances, such as concerts or theater productions, where quantum entanglement enables attendees from around the world to experience the event simultaneously as if they were physically present together. Imagine attending a performance where not only visual and auditory experiences are transmitted seamlessly but emotional and sensory engagements are facilitated through quantum-enhanced platforms. Each participant would perceive the atmosphere—the excitement, energy, and reactions of fellow attendees—creating a shared experience that fosters a sense of community and connection absent in traditional streaming approaches.

Furthermore, the potential for interactive storytelling takes on an entirely new dimension with the adoption of Quantum Proxy technologies. Imagine a narrative where viewers can influence plot directions in real-time, engaging with characters and each other in a shared immersive environment. By leveraging quantum principles, creators could harness the collective input of participants, weaving their decisions into the narrative fabric, thus crafting a unique storytelling experience that feels deeply resonant and authentic. This participatory model could redefine media consumption, shifting the audience from passive viewers to active contributors, thereby enriching the narrative itself.

The introduction of Quantum Proxy holds implications for various facets of the entertainment industry, including gaming, virtual and augmented reality experiences, and even digital content creation. In gaming, the capacity for real-time interactions driven by quantum entanglement may allow players to experience interconnected gameplay across geographic divides, fostering unparalleled engagement and collaboration. Multiplayer online games could evolve into immersive experiences where players navigate shared spaces, strategizing and communicating intuitively as though they were physically situated together.

Moreover, as media organizations seek to innovate within the competitive landscape, the integration of Quantum Proxy offers practical solutions to common challenges. Traditional content distribution methods often encounter hurdles such as bandwidth limitations and content delivery delays, which can hinder the user experience. Quantum-enhanced communication networks can enhance content delivery systems by ensuring that media content is transmitted securely and instantaneously, allowing audiences to access high-quality content without interruption or degradation in quality.

The implications of Quantum Proxy for media and entertainment extend into the realm of accessibility as well. The ability to create immersive, quantum-enabled experiences could democratize access to cultural events, theatrical performances, and live concerts for audiences who may face geographical constraints, financial barriers, or mobility challenges. As media organizations facilitate equitable access and representation, they can foster a more inclusive and diverse entertainment landscape, ensuring that varied voices and experiences are embraced and celebrated.

However, the adoption of Quantum Proxy in media and entertainment is not without its challenges. As we navigate the potential benefits, we must also critically consider the ethical ramifications surrounding privacy, data protection, and content ownership. The shared experiences facilitated through quantum technologies raise questions about data collection, user consent, and the implications of surveillance in hyper-connected virtual environments. Safeguarding individual rights while promoting innovation will be vital as the boundaries between the physical and digital become increasingly blurred.

Moreover, as we explore the possibilities for Quantum Proxy, the entertainment industry must consider the impact on existing revenue models and content creation practices. The shift toward quantum-enhanced media experiences may disrupt traditional financial structures, prompting a reevaluation of monetization strategies in an era where access and engagement take center stage.

In summary, the impacts of Quantum Proxy on media and entertainment present a kaleidoscope of possibilities that challenge conventional paradigms. By harnessing the principles of quantum mechanics, the potential for real-time interactions, immersive storytelling, and equitable access to cultural experiences redefines how audiences engage with media. As we envision a future where quantum technologies play an integral role in entertainment, it is essential to create ethical frameworks and dialogue that prioritize individual rights, inclusivity, and equitable access. The unfolding journey into this quantum-enhanced landscape promises to reshape our experiences, fostering deeper connections between creators, audiences, and communities in ways previously confined to the realm of imagination.

8.5. Case Study: Quantum Communication Breakthroughs

The landscape of quantum communication breakthroughs presents a fascinating case study that embodies the groundbreaking advances being made within the field of Quantum Proxy. These breakthroughs showcase the transformative potential of quantum mechanics applied to communication technologies, illustrating how they can fundamentally reshape human interaction, connectivity, and even our understanding of presence.

To begin with, one notable breakthrough was the successful demonstration of quantum key distribution (QKD) over long distances using satellite technology. In 2017, the Chinese satellite Micius was launched as part of a pioneering research initiative to test the feasibility of QKD in real-world conditions. By employing a satellite to transmit entangled photon pairs across hundreds of kilometers, researchers were able to establish a secure quantum communication channel between distant locations. This landmark achievement exemplifies the promise of quantum technologies for secure data transmission and sets the stage for future applications of Quantum Proxy in various sectors, including government communications, finance, and critical infrastructure.

In another remarkable case, researchers at the University of Science and Technology of China conducted experiments that achieved quantum teleportation across a distance of more than 500 kilometers. This breakthrough involved the teleportation of quantum information via a technique that efficiently utilized entangled particles. The implications for Quantum Proxy are tremendous; by demonstrating the capability of teleporting quantum states over significant distances, researchers opened up avenues for potential real-time remote interactions that capitalize on quantum entanglement's non-local attributes. Such advancements pave the way for establishing instantaneous telepresence experiences, where individuals can engage across vast spatial separations and feel intimately connected.

Additionally, the development of quantum repeaters has emerged as a crucial factor in extending the reach of quantum communication networks. These devices facilitate the preservation of entanglement over longer distances by amplifying quantum signals and minimizing the effects of decoherence that threaten quantum states. A multi-institutional collaborative effort has led to breakthroughs in designing advanced quantum repeater systems that can seamlessly integrate into future quantum communication networks. The ability to maintain entangled particles over long distances is paramount for realizing Quantum Proxy at a global scale, where real-time connectivity becomes a transformative reality.

Moreover, initiatives at institutions like IBM and Google signify a surge in interest surrounding quantum computing's capabilities and its implications for communication. IBM's Quantum Experience allows users worldwide to access their quantum processors, encouraging exploration and experimentation in quantum algorithms. As quantum computing matures, the intersection of quantum computing and communication offers exciting possibilities for enhancing the performance of Quantum Proxy, enabling immediate data processing on an unparalleled scale. The collaboration between quantum computing and communication technologies offers the prospect of seamlessly integrating telepresence into everyday interactions, enriching experiences through enhanced computational power.

Collaborative efforts across global frontiers comprise an essential component of the advances in quantum communication. International collaborations, such as the Quantum Internet Alliance, aim to bring together researchers and institutions to develop a quantum internet built on principles of entanglement and superposition. The Alliance works on building protocols to establish quantum communication networks, share resources, and progress toward quantum communication on a global scale by fostering partnerships that play to the strengths of various institutions and experts.

As we examine the future directions and unanswered questions in quantum communication breakthroughs, several exciting possibilities emerge. Key research could focus on the challenge of scalability —addressing how to maintain coherence and security as quantum communication systems expand. Further exploration of error correction techniques will be crucial in ensuring the reliability of quantum channels over increased distances. Additionally, understanding the nuances of integrating quantum communication within existing infrastructures raises questions of how traditional communication systems could adapt and evolve in tandem with emerging quantum technologies.

The case study of quantum communication breakthroughs highlights the transformative potential of Quantum Proxy. By showcasing successful implementations, collaborative research initiatives, and the practical feasibility of quantum communication, we gain insight into the future possibilities that await. The journey towards realizing Quantum Proxy is characterized by a commitment to innovating and addressing the ethical implications that arise along the way.

As researchers and technologists collaborate to push the boundaries of what is possible in quantum communication, we stand on the precipice of a new era where connectivity knows no limits and human experiences are enriched beyond imagination. The exploration of quantum communication breakthroughs not only captures the current advancements but also serves as a testament to a collective commitment to paving the way for a more interconnected and enriched human experience.

9. Research Frontiers in Quantum Proxy

9.1. Current Trends in Quantum Research

The field of quantum research is currently experiencing a renaissance, marked by groundbreaking discoveries and technological advancements that promise to shift our understanding and applications of quantum mechanics in the realm of communication and beyond. As we delve into current trends in quantum research, it is essential to recognize how these developments underpin the feasibility of concepts such as Quantum Proxy—the potential for telepresence through quantum entanglement.

Key areas in quantum research include enhanced quantum communication, quantum computing, and the explorations of entanglement's applications. Researchers are increasingly utilizing quantum mechanics to address the limitations of classical communication, particularly focusing on how quantum states can be harnessed for instantaneous information transfer. One prominent trend is the ongoing improvement in quantum key distribution techniques (QKD) that secure communications against eavesdropping. As these methods gain sophistication, they provide a robust foundation for secure data transmission, crucial for implementing technologies that hinge on telepresence.

Particularly noteworthy is the trend of exploring quantum entanglement beyond mere theoretical constructs. Researchers are uncovering practical applications that leverage entangled particles for more than just secure key distribution. For example, the advancements in quantum teleportation—where quantum information can be transmitted instantaneously over distances without physical particle movement—demonstrate how entanglement can facilitate real-time interaction across vast separations. This empirical progress lays groundwork for Quantum Proxy, as it shows the functionality of quantum mechanics in enabling experiences that transcend conventional limits.

Internationally, quantum research initiatives are on the rise as nations recognize the strategic importance of quantum technology.

Governments and organizations are pouring resources into quantum research, signaling a global race to leverage quantum mechanics for various applications that could revolutionize industries. Initiatives such as the European Quantum Technologies Flagship and the United States' National Quantum Initiative serve as catalysts for collaboration across academia, industry, and policy-making, each aiming to propel quantum research into practical implementation. This commitment to advancing quantum technologies emphasizes the collective recognition of their transformative potential on a global scale.

Many pioneering institutions contribute to advancements in quantum research. For example, leading universities and national laboratories have emerged as frontiers for innovative explorations into quantum phenomena. These institutions are often at the helm of developing new technologies and experimental methods, focusing on enhancing quantum communication systems, characterizing qubits, and understanding the implications of entangled states. By fostering interdisciplinary collaborations among physicists, engineers, and computer scientists, these institutions play a critical role in translating quantum concepts into applications that can reshape communication and telepresence.

Collaboration is a recurring theme in current quantum research, as international partnerships enhance the scope and impact of various projects. Nations are increasingly recognizing that many challenges require collective expertise, as evidenced by collaborative efforts like the Quantum Internet Alliance and International Quantum Communications initiatives. These alliances encourage shared resources, knowledge exchanges, and research pooling, ultimately driving further innovations in the quantum field. By working together, international research initiatives can tackle complex challenges such as maintaining entanglement over long distances and developing successful error correction techniques, thereby forging a shared path toward practical implementations of Quantum Proxy.

Looking into the future, several unanswered questions remain about quantum communication and entanglement applications. One critical area of research is scalability. While significant strides have been made experimentally, understanding how to maintain quantum coherence and effectively integrate quantum communication systems within existing networks remains pivotal for widespread application. Researchers also continue to explore diverse applications—from quantum computing capabilities to advancements in navigation and space exploration—that might arise from utilizing quantum mechanics more broadly.

In summary, current trends in quantum research reveal an invigorated discipline poised to usher in transformative technologies. As significant breakthroughs continue to emerge in quantum communication, entanglement applications, and collaborative initiatives, the groundwork is being laid for realizing Quantum Proxy. This promise of telepresence through quantum entanglement represents not only a technological leap but a potential redefinition of how we connect and interact across distances. As the global scientific community continues to explore the vast potential of quantum mechanics, the prospects for enhancing communication through these advancements will undoubtedly shape the future of human experience and connectivity. The ongoing journey through the quantum frontier transforms possibilities into realities, stretching our imagination toward a future where instant presence is no longer confined to the realm of science fiction but becomes an integral part of our everyday lives.

9.2. Global Research Initiatives

In the contemporary landscape of scientific inquiry, global research initiatives are forging pathways into the uncharted territory of quantum capabilities, particularly as they relate to Quantum Proxy—the pioneering concept of telepresence through quantum entanglement. This subchapter examines the diverse spectrum of research efforts occurring across borders, highlighting not only the advancements being made but also the collaborative spirit that underpins these dynamic undertakings.

The field of quantum research has witnessed a notable surge in global interest, driven by the realization that quantum technology harbors transformative potential across a myriad of domains, including communication, computing, cryptography, and beyond. As nations recognize the strategic importance of quantum capabilities, research institutions, governments, and industries are aligning objectives to cultivate an ecosystem primed for advancement. Efforts to harness quantum mechanics for real-world applications have become increasingly multidimensional, relying on collaborative frameworks that prioritize the joint expertise of scientists and engineers around the globe.

Among the most significant developments in recent years is the establishment of international research consortia focused on quantum technologies. Published studies, joint projects, and initiatives have proliferated as scientists share knowledge, expertise, and resources worldwide to address complex challenges associated with quantum entanglement, secure communication, and computational frameworks. Research institutions like the Massachusetts Institute of Technology (MIT), the University of Science and Technology of China (USTC), and the European Organization for Nuclear Research (CERN) are collaborating with partners worldwide to develop next-generation quantum communication networks.

Highlighting this collaborative spirit is the Quantum Internet Alliance, which mobilizes research leaders and institutions across Europe to construct the foundations of a secure quantum internet. This ambitious initiative aims to develop protocols and systems for quantum communication that can be integrated with existing classical networks. By pooling resources and expertise, the Quantum Internet Alliance serves as a blueprint for how research entities can work together to enhance the development of quantum technologies, thereby accelerating progress in telepresence capabilities offered by Quantum Proxy.

Complementing these initiatives are government-sponsored programs and funding schemes aimed at fostering future generations of quantum research. In the United States, for instance, the National Quantum Initiative seeks to bolster national quantum research efforts with a focus on collaboration between academia, government laboratories, and industry players. Similar initiatives can be observed in countries such as China, Canada, and the European Union, where governments are investing heavily in quantum research through national research foundations and high-tech strategy initiatives. This convergence fosters momentum toward achieving breakthroughs that directly contribute to the practical viability of concepts like Quantum Proxy.

As global partnerships coalesce around quantum research, specific challenges have emerged as pressing focal points for inquiry. The maintenance of quantum entanglement over long distances, the effects of decoherence, and the development of scalable quantum communication networks remain pivotal questions that researchers are actively investigating. Collaborative efforts across countries are critical for addressing these challenges, as shared research outcomes can lead to the formulation of robust solutions drawn from diverse theoretical and experimental perspectives. Inter-institutional dialogues ensure that researchers remain aligned and responsive to the evolving landscape of quantum capabilities.

Conversely, these collaborative efforts raise ethical considerations and questions of governance surrounding the implications of quantum technologies. As research initiatives proliferate, the accompanying discourse about the ethical use of quantum capabilities—specifically in the realm of privacy, security, and equity—has gained traction. Engaging with these issues on a global scale allows researchers to foster responsible innovation that prioritizes consensus-building, ensuring that the benefits of quantum technologies are equitably distributed while upholding ethical standards.

As we peer into future directions for global research initiatives, unanswered questions surrounding the scalability of quantum systems and their fusion with existing communication infrastructures emerge as focal areas for continued exploration. The advancement of quantum communication presents prospects for not only enhancing stability and connectivity but also for redefining what is possible in virtual engagement, ultimately catalyzing the realization of Quantum Proxy capabilities.

In conclusion, global research initiatives in quantum technologies represent a tapestry woven from diverse contributions, collaborative efforts, and a shared commitment to exploring the transformative potential of quantum mechanics. As nations and institutions come together to collectively tackle the challenges presented by quantum capabilities, the pathways toward realizing concepts like Quantum Proxy become clearer. Enhanced international cooperation enables accelerated progress, driving innovations that promise to reshape our understanding of communication, presence, and connection as we navigate the quantum frontier.

9.3. Pioneering Institutions and Their Contributions

The advancement of communication technologies, particularly through the lens of quantum mechanics, has seen a surge of interest from pioneering institutions around the world, each contributing uniquely to the growing body of knowledge. The phenomenon of Quantum Proxy—utilizing quantum entanglement for telepresence—hinges on foundational contributions from various research entities that have shaped our understanding and implementation of quantum principles in practical scenarios.

At the forefront of this quantum revolution are institutions like the Massachusetts Institute of Technology (MIT), California Institute of Technology (Caltech), and universities in China, such as Tsinghua University and the University of Science and Technology of China (USTC). These institutions have established world-renowned research programs dedicated to exploring the myriad applications of quantum mechanics. Their contributions span innovations in quantum cryptography, communication protocols, and error correction techniques, all central to the realization of secure quantum networks.

For instance, MIT has played a critical role in developing quantum key distribution (QKD) systems, which safeguard quantum communication through entangled particles. By establishing protocols to detect potential eavesdropping, MIT's research has directly influenced how secure communications could function in real-world applications, paving the way for technologies that reinforce user trust in remote interactions. Similarly, researchers at Caltech have focused on integrating quantum communication with classical networks, articulating the frameworks necessary to ensure seamless connectivity between the two realms.

The University of Science and Technology of China (USTC) has also made groundbreaking contributions to quantum communication research. Their 2017 launch of the Micius satellite marked a pivotal moment in demonstrating the feasibility of satellite-based quantum communication, achieving secure transmission of quantum keys over gigabits per second. This achievement not only highlights the potential applications of quantum technologies in secure communication but also sets the stage for transforming how we think about distance, data integrity, and telepresence.

Moreover, international collaborations have fostered advancements that reach beyond individual institutions, enhancing the quantum research landscape collaboratively. Initiatives like the Quantum Internet Alliance bring together experts from various countries to establish protocols and frameworks for quantum networks. This collective effort underscores the realization that the future of quantum capabilities must be forged through shared knowledge, intercultural exchange, and mutual support among nations.

The confluence of ideas generated by such collaborative efforts has illuminated potential advancements across sectors. For instance, quantum mechanics' application in healthcare has been explored vigorously, given its potential to usher in sophisticated models for patient data privacy and secure medical communications. Harnessing Quantum Proxy technologies could enable remote consultations that feel entirely immersive, allowing healthcare professionals to engage with patients emotionally and physically, despite geographical barriers.

In education, the integration of quantum technologies into curricula stands to redefine learning paradigms. Institutions investing in quantum education create environments where students interactively engage with quantum mechanics through experiments and virtual simulations, preparing a future workforce adept in quantum technologies and their applications. The potential for enriched learning experiences through Quantum Proxy would enable educators to break geographical barriers, enhancing collaboration and knowledge exchange across diverse educational landscapes.

As pioneering institutions lead the charge within specific domains, the anticipated outcomes of leveraging Quantum Proxy across industries are profound. In manufacturing, the precision offered by quantum sensors can significantly enhance operational efficiencies, ultimately streamlining supply chains and production processes. In space exploration, quantum navigation could revolutionize how we traverse and map vast distances, providing insights into compartmentalized data derived from satellite technologies enhanced by quantum communication.

In conclusion, the contributions of pioneering institutions globally are critical to unlocking the transformative potential of Quantum Proxy and its applications in communication technologies. These collective efforts yield valuable knowledge, ensuring that quantum frameworks and protocols can be integrated into real-world applications, ultimately reshaping our understanding of communication itself. As we continue to chart our course through the complexities of quantum mechanics and its implications for society, these institutions remain pivotal to our journey toward realizing a future characterized by enhanced connections and the redefinition of human experience through quantum entanglement.

9.4. Collaborative Efforts Across Borders

In an increasingly interconnected world where technological advancements unfold at a dizzying pace, the collaboration of global efforts across borders becomes vital in unlocking the potential of quantum technologies, particularly in the context of Quantum Proxy. This emerging field, which promises to redefine communication through telepresence enabled by quantum entanglement, has garnered attention from researchers, institutions, and governments worldwide. As we delve into the collaborative endeavors shaping this new frontier, we recognize the richness that diversity of thought and expertise brings to addressing complex questions that transcend geographical boundaries.

The phenomenon of quantum mechanics is inherently universal, inviting contributions from various cultures and scientific traditions. Pioneering institutions from North America, Europe, and Asia have joined forces to push the boundaries of what is possible. For instance, the establishment of extensive research networks—like the European Quantum Technologies Flagship and the National Quantum Initiative in the United States—has created platforms for collaboration that span continents. These initiatives encourage institutions to share resources, best practices, and experimental findings, fostering an environment of mutual support essential for tackling the outstanding challenges inherent to quantum technology development.

Joint research projects not only enhance intellectual capital but also help standardize protocols and methodologies, paving the road for more reliable implementations of quantum communication technologies. Collaborative work on quantum key distribution (QKD) is a prime example, where findings from various countries have culminated in unified strategies to develop encryption frameworks that are secure against eavesdropping. These efforts draw upon the collective expertise found in diverse academic and industrial settings, ensuring that quantum communication systems are resilient and effective.

A compelling instance of cross-border collaboration is witnessed in the quantum internet initiatives gaining traction globally. Countries such as China, the United States, Canada, and members of the European Union have committed to building quantum communication networks that harness the full power of entanglement, ensuring secure interactions at unprecedented speeds. By sharing technological advancements and engaging in joint experiments, researchers can tackle the engineering hurdles associated with creating reliable, large-scale quantum networks, ultimately aspiring toward the realization of the Quantum Internet.

However, the journey toward conceptualizing and implementing Quantum Proxy is not without challenges. For instance, researchers continue to grapple with the phenomena of decoherence, where quantum states interact with their environment, potentially leading to loss of information. Collaborative efforts are crucial to establishing methods of isolating quantum systems from environmental interference, reducing the risk of decoherence. By bringing together experts from different fields—such as materials science, engineering, and quantum physics—interdisciplinary projects can emerge that expedite research and development, producing innovations that may significantly enhance the viability of quantum communication systems.

In addition, ethical considerations concerning the deployment of quantum technologies arise as significant points of inquiry in collaborative initiatives. Questions surrounding privacy, surveillance, and equitable access become heightened in discussions that engage diverse perspectives. Cross-border collaborations provide invaluable opportunities to exchange ideas about setting international standards and regulations that govern the use of quantum technology, ensuring that ethical frameworks align with technological advancement to safeguard individual rights and promote social equity.

Establishing academic and industry partnerships across borders can also enrich educational frameworks, preparing a future workforce equipped with the necessary skills to navigate the intricacies of quantum mechanics. Collaborative training programs focused on quantum technologies facilitate international exchanges, where students from disparate backgrounds come together to learn, solve problems, and explore the diverse applications of quantum principles. By fostering such interactions in academia, institutions can cultivate a global community of thinkers who can innovate collectively and holistically address pressing challenges in the quantum realm.

As we stand at the intersection of quantum mechanics and daily life, the collaborative efforts across borders signify a collective ambition to uncover the transformative potential locked within Quantum Proxy. From joint experiments to shared visions and ethical discussions, these endeavors illuminate the paths forward, ensuring that the benefits of quantum technologies reach fruition. The future of communication, enabled by quantum entanglement, beckons us toward a horizon where distance is trivial, and human experiences are enhanced through rich interactions that resonate across the globe.

In exploring future directions and unanswered questions that lie beyond the horizon of current advancements, we envision a world enhanced by quantum capabilities, bridging the distances that have traditionally defined our relationships and communications. As our understanding of quantum principles deepens, new dimensions of inquiry emerge, prompting further investigations into the implications of Quantum Proxy technologies across various fields, thus setting the stage for an extraordinary journey ahead.

9.5. Future Directions and Unanswered Questions

In today's rapidly advancing technological landscape, the potential for Quantum Proxy to reshape communication and interaction is accompanied by an array of future directions and unanswered questions. As researchers and practitioners delve deeper into the principles and applications of quantum mechanics, it becomes increasingly critical to explore not only the advancements but also the implications that these transformative technologies may have across diverse fields.

One crucial area ripe for exploration is the medical field. Quantum technologies hold the promise of revolutionizing healthcare through advancements in diagnostics and treatment methodologies. For instance, researchers are already investigating the application of quantum sensors to enhance imaging techniques, enabling the capture of high-resolution images that could lead to faster disease diagnosis. Furthermore, the potential for secure telemedicine consultations, powered by entangled particles, could allow healthcare professionals to share sensitive patient data with the utmost security, thus building trust in digital interactions. However, significant questions remain regarding the integration of these technologies into existing medical frameworks and the regulatory processes that will govern their widespread adoption.

Similarly, the intersection of quantum computing and artificial intelligence offers a treasure trove of potential applications. As quantum computing continues to evolve, it could unlock new algorithms that dramatically enhance machine learning capabilities, leading to unprecedented advancements in decision-making, problem-solving, and data analysis. The ability of quantum computers to process vast amounts of data at lightning speed raises compelling questions about the future of AI systems and how they integrate with our daily lives. What ethical considerations must be addressed as AI and quantum computing converge? How will this shift affect employment and the nature of work? Exploring these questions will be vital to ensuring a balanced view of the benefits and challenges ahead.

Education and learning represent another fertile ground for the application of quantum technologies. The potential for immersive educational experiences wherein students can engage with quantum principles in real time can redefine the learning landscape. Quantum Proxy could enable dynamic classrooms where students from all over the world participate collaboratively in virtual experiments and lectures, guided by experts. This opens up engaging opportunities for cross-cultural educational exchanges, but it also necessitates addressing issues of accessibility and equity to prevent the digital divide from widening further.

Furthermore, the manufacturing and industrial sector stands to benefit profoundly from adopting quantum technologies. The ability to utilize quantum mechanics for optimizing supply chains, improving production efficiency, and enabling predictive maintenance demonstrates the transformative impact on industrial operations. How will industries adapt to incorporate these technologies, and what will this shift mean for labor practices and workforce training? These are critical considerations for understanding the broader implications of quantum advancements.

Quantum navigation and space exploration represent yet another expansive domain impacted by quantum technologies. The application of quantum sensors in the exploration of celestial bodies holds promise for significantly improving our capabilities in space travel and mapping the universe. Questions surrounding the feasibility of implementing these systems in space missions, as well as their potential challenges, should be examined to harness the full benefits of quantum technology for space exploration.

As we envision the future of Quantum Proxy, we must also consider the pathway from concept to reality. The development of quantum technologies necessitates ongoing interdisciplinary collaboration and collective action to enhance our understanding and address the technical challenges. The establishment of a quantum-centric approach to communication will involve integrating existing systems with quantum capabilities, fostering a hybrid landscape that capitalizes on the unique benefits that quantum mechanics brings without dismissing classical methods.

Moreover, the quest for quantum ubiquity—where quantum communication is seamlessly integrated into daily life—requires sustained research and investment. The path to achieving this vision may include not only technological breakthroughs but also regulatory frameworks that ensure privacy, accessibility, and ethical practices. The engagement of stakeholders, policymakers, scientists, and the public in discussions surrounding these themes will be crucial in shaping the future of quantum-enhanced communication.

The journey into the future, driven by the principles of quantum mechanics, extends far beyond the material implications of technology. It calls for a reevaluation of what it means to connect with one another and the nature of human interaction itself. As Quantum Proxy capabilities flourish, we find ourselves on the cusp of a redefined understanding of presence, intimacy, and the ways we share our lives with others. Through collaborations that embrace diversity, innovation, and inclusivity, we can begin to craft a future where quantum technologies foster richer human experiences, transcending geographical barriers and enabling unparalleled connections across the globe.

However, with these exciting advancements comes the responsibility to navigate the ethical complexities and challenges that may arise. Continuous reflection on the implications of Quantum Proxy technologies—and a commitment to ensuring equitable access and ethical governance—will ultimately determine the impact and character of this new era. As we stand poised at the brink of unprecedented possibilities, the collective choices we make today will shape not only the future of quantum communication but the broader relationship between technology and the human experience. Embracing this journey with intention and thoughtfulness will pave the way for a reality that enhances our interconnectedness while safeguarding our fundamental values and rights.

10. Potential Applications in Various Fields

10.1. Medical Advancements through Quantum Technologies

As we stand on the precipice of a new era defined by technological innovation and scientific promise, it is imperative to consider the potential applications of quantum technologies across various fields. Among these emerging opportunities, medical advancements through quantum technologies represent a particularly noteworthy area, with the capacity to revolutionize healthcare delivery, diagnostics, treatment methodologies, and patient outcomes.

The intersection of quantum mechanics and medicine has already yielded promising discoveries in areas such as imaging, information security, and drug development. One key application lies in the enhancement of medical imaging techniques through advanced quantum sensors. These sensors capitalize on the unique sensitivity of quantum states, allowing for the detection of minute changes in biological signals that traditional imaging methods may not identify. By harnessing entangled particles and superposition, positions, energies, and metabolic markers can be visualized with unprecedented resolution, fundamentally altering the diagnostic landscape.

Consider the implications of using quantum-enhanced magnetic resonance imaging (MRI) or quantum ultrasound to create detailed and dynamic images of tissues and organs. Such breakthroughs could significantly expedite the detection of diseases such as cancer and neurological disorders, enabling timely and targeted interventions that ultimately improve patient outcomes. Furthermore, the ability to monitor real-time physiological changes could pave the way for personalized medicine, where treatments are tailored to individual patients based on their specific health profiles revealed through advanced imaging.

In addition to diagnostics, quantum technologies hold great potential in drug discovery and development. The complexities of molecular behavior and interactions can be modeled more accurately using quantum simulations, enabling researchers to identify potential drug candidates and predict their effects with greater precision. By tapping into quantum computing capabilities, researchers could expedite the drug development process, thereby reducing the time and resources needed to bring new therapies to market. As quantum algorithms advance, the intricacies of biochemical interactions may be deciphered more efficiently, addressing pressing health challenges with agility and innovation.

One must also consider the ethical implications of introducing quantum technologies into the medical arena. As the sophistication of medical tools increases, so too does the importance of securing patient data and ensuring compliance with privacy standards. Quantum key distribution (QKD) can fortify the security of sensitive information transmitted during telemedicine consultations, safeguarding patient confidentiality even in a digitally connected world. This interplay between quantum communication and healthcare paves the way for establishing trust in telehealth solutions, especially important in a time when remote access to care is becoming the norm.

The potential for quantum technologies to facilitate telemedicine is profound. Through the lens of Quantum Proxy, imagine real-time consultations between healthcare professionals and patients, where both parties could share immersive experiences that feel as authentic as in-person visits. Utilizing quantum entanglement, doctors could engage with patients dynamically, analyzing data collaboratively and reaching informed conclusions that drive treatment decisions. The reduction of geographical barriers in accessing healthcare services emphasizes the transformative power of quantum technologies in elevating health equity for underserved populations.

The combined benefits of enhanced diagnostics, personalized medicine, and secure telehealth illustrate the breadth of quantum advancements in medicine, reinforcing a vision where healthcare delivery is revolutionized. As we navigate the intersection of quantum principles and medical innovation, crucial questions arise about the role of interdisciplinary collaborations among physicists, biomedical researchers, and healthcare professionals. Fostering such partnerships will be essential for harmonizing technological advancements with clinical applications, ensuring that the transformative potential of quantum technologies is realized for the benefit of society.

In summary, the prospect of medical advancements through quantum technologies is a thrilling facet of the broader implications tied to Quantum Proxy. The possibilities for enhanced imaging, precision medicine, and secure communication are only the beginning of what quantum innovations can achieve in the healthcare domain. As we look toward this promising future, we must remain vigilant about accompanying ethical considerations, ensuring that the transformative power of quantum technologies is harnessed responsibly, with a commitment to patient-centered care and health equity woven into the fabric of our healthcare systems. The convergence of science and medicine, magnified through the lens of quantum mechanics, beckons us to an era where the boundaries of possibility expand and human health is elevated through the extraordinary capabilities of quantum technologies.

10.2. Quantum Computing and Artificial Intelligence

In the age of rapid technological advancement, the intersection of quantum mechanics and artificial intelligence (AI) exemplifies one of the most promising frontiers in science and technology. The convergence of these two fields not only enhances computational capabilities but also presents revolutionary pathways for developing effective quantum systems and algorithms. As we examine the relationship between quantum computing and AI, we delve into the potential applications, strengths, and transformative impacts they might have across numerous domains—ultimately supporting the realization of concepts like Quantum Proxy.

Quantum computing, characterized by its ability to process vast amounts of data through the manipulation of quantum bits (qubits) that can exist in multiple states simultaneously, stands poised to enhance AI architectures dramatically. Where classical computers operate within deterministic frameworks, quantum systems leverage superposition and entanglement to explore solutions exponentially faster than their classical counterparts. This capability is particularly relevant for AI applications, which often require complex computations and analyses.

One of the most profound implications of this convergence is in optimizing machine learning algorithms. Quantum computing can enable substantially more efficient training of AI models. For instance, quantum algorithms can handle vast training sets without the prohibitive time costs that classical models incur. Quantum-enhanced machine learning (QML) has the potential to revolutionize areas such as image recognition, natural language processing, and predictive analytics, where the need for accuracy and speed becomes paramount. Utilizing quantum systems, AI could achieve levels of precision previously deemed unattainable in real-time decision-making scenarios.

Additionally, quantum computing can redefine how AI systems process and analyze data patterns. Traditional machine learning approaches often rely on classical probabilistic inferencing methods that involve assumptions about the data distribution. By harnessing quantum principles, AI can explore multidimensional data relationships without making such assumptions, revealing hidden patterns and correlations within datasets. This enhanced understanding can lead to more accurate predictions and improved datasets, ultimately refining the output of AI applications across sectors like finance, healthcare, and climate modeling.

Furthermore, as AI and quantum technologies seamlessly integrate, the potential for real-time analysis and adaptability within dynamic environments grows exponentially. For instance, consider a scenario in financial markets where instant data processing, made possible by quantum computing, enables AI systems to adapt trading algorithms in response to market fluctuations. The combination of quantum computing and AI would allow for rapid decision-making based on up-to-the-minute data, facilitating more agile financial strategies.

Moreover, the implications of coupling AI with quantum systems extend into the realm of automation and robotics. Quantum-enhanced AI can facilitate the development of advanced robotic systems capable of performing complex tasks in real-world scenarios. This fusion can lead to substantial improvements in sectors like manufacturing, logistics, and autonomous vehicles—where AI systems guided by quantum-computed analyses can make decisions and adapt nimbly to changing conditions.

The collaborative efforts between quantum researchers and AI specialists demonstrate growing recognition of the importance of interdisciplinary research. Initiatives that merge expertise from both fields are essential for realizing the potential benefits of their integration. Moreover, as we explore this convergence, it is crucial to address any ethical implications associated with the adoption of such advanced technologies. Transparency in AI decision-making, ensuring equitable access to quantum-enhanced applications, and addressing privacy concerns must be pivotal in guiding the development of this transformative relationship.

As we navigate the unfolding relationship between quantum computing and AI, the future promises exciting possibilities. Quantum Proxy serves as a illustration of how this convergence can reshape communication, enhancing our ability to connect with others in ways that transcend current limitations. The pathways toward real-time telepresence defined by instant interactions and emotional resonance can be intricately supported by the strengths of quantum computing partners in AI systems.

In conclusion, the synergy between quantum computing and artificial intelligence illuminates immense potential for transformation. By harnessing the unique attributes of quantum systems, AI applications can experience unprecedented advancements in their processing, adaptability, and efficiency. As we chart our trajectory toward realizing the ambitions of Quantum Proxy, the role of quantum computing and AI stands as a testament to the incredible possibilities lying ahead in reimagining human experience, connectivity, and interaction. The journey offers a glimpse into a future where barriers dissolve, and we engage with technology in ways that feel immediate, authentic, and deeply resonant.

10.3. Impact on Education and Learning

The advancements in quantum mechanics, particularly the concept of Quantum Proxy, has the potential to reshape the landscape of education and learning profoundly. As quantum technologies evolve, they can facilitate innovative approaches to knowledge dissemination, experiential learning, and collaborative engagement, providing opportunities to overcome traditional barriers in education.

At the heart of this transformation is the ability of Quantum Proxy to enable real-time, immersive, and interactive communication. By leveraging the properties of quantum entanglement, educators can create learning environments that transcend geographical constraints, allowing students from diverse backgrounds to engage with experts and peers worldwide. Imagine classrooms where students in remote locations can participate in lectures delivered by renowned scholars in real time, experiencing discussions, insights, and mentorship that would otherwise be inaccessible. This paradigm shift signifies a democratization of education, where knowledge flows freely across borders, fostering a global community of learners.

The enhancement of virtual learning experiences through quantum technologies could also elevate engagement levels among students. Traditional methods of education, while effective, often rely heavily on passive consumption of information—often through lectures or textbook readings. Quantum Proxy technologies can transform this dynamic, enabling experiential learning opportunities that allow students to interact directly with concepts and materials. For instance, students could engage in dynamic simulations driven by quantum principles, allowing them to manipulate variables and observe outcomes in real time. Such immersive experiences stimulate curiosity, promote critical thinking, and provide hands-on learning that resonates with diverse learning styles.

Moreover, the potential for collaboration among students situated in different parts of the world can lead to enriched cultural exchanges and global dialogues. Imagine students from various countries cooperating on collaborative projects, sharing insights, and tackling global challenges collectively. Leveraging quantum-enabled platforms, these interactions would foster cross-cultural understanding, empathy, and a deeper appreciation of diverse perspectives—elements critical for navigating the complexities of an interconnected world.

The integration of quantum technologies into educational frameworks also invites opportunities for personalized learning experiences. AI-driven quantum systems can assess individual student learning styles, performance metrics, and preferences, tailoring educational content to meet specific needs. This customization empowers learners to progress at their own pace, enhancing retention and mastery of complex concepts—a departure from one-size-fits-all approaches that often leave students behind.

Furthermore, the implications of quantum-enhanced education extend into assessment methods. Traditional examinations and evaluations have inherent limitations in assessing a student's understanding. Quantum technologies can facilitate innovative assessment models that prioritize formative feedback, allowing educators to gauge student grasp of topics continuously. By leveraging real-time data analytics and student engagement metrics captured through quantum communication, educators can adapt their instructional approaches to align with students' progress effectively.

Despite the immense promise of quantum-enhanced education, challenges remain. The accessibility of quantum technologies will determine how equitable this transformation becomes. As educational institutions and governments work to implement quantum infrastructure, ensuring that all students have access to these resources is essential. Initiatives aimed at democratizing quantum education will be vital to preventing exacerbation of existing inequalities. The focus should be on integrating quantum principles into curricula while providing teachers with adequate training and resources to utilize these tools effectively.

As we envision the future impact of Quantum Proxy technologies on education and learning, we see an opportunity to foster richer, more authentic learning experiences that resonate with diverse student populations. By marrying quantum communication with educational innovation, we can catalyze a shift towards a more connected, collaborative, and inclusive learning environment. The potential for Quantum Proxy to dissolve traditional barriers in education fosters a vision where knowledge is democratized, engagement is elevated, and every learner has an equal opportunity to thrive in a globalized society.

In summary, the implications of Quantum Proxy for education encompass heightened engagement, personalized learning, and enhanced collaboration across borders. As we embrace this transformative potential, we must remain vigilant about the challenges surrounding accessibility and inequality, ensuring that the benefits of quantum technologies are equitably distributed among all students. By fostering an educational landscape enriched by quantum innovation, we embark on a journey toward a future where knowledge is freed from constraints, enabling deeper connections and broader horizons for learners worldwide. The evolution of education through Quantum Proxy heralds a new era of possibility, paving the way for empowered minds to collaboratively innovate and shape the future.

10.4. Manufacturing and Industrial Efficiency

The roots of modern manufacturing and industrial efficiency may well lie in how we effectively harness technological advancements, particularly those driven by quantum mechanics. In the exploration of efficiencies within this realm, Quantum Proxy emerges as a beacon of transformative potential, promising to redefine the ways we approach manufacturing processes, supply chain management, and overall production capabilities.

The integration of quantum communication technologies is set to revolutionize how industries operate. As organizations increasingly rely on interconnected systems for managing resources and operations, the potential for instantaneous information sharing facilitated by Quantum Proxy becomes clear. By leveraging quantum entanglement, data can be transmitted securely and in real-time across vast distances, allowing different facilities, suppliers, and manufacturers to communicate fluidly, irrespective of geographical constraints. This level of connectivity can drastically enhance decision-making processes, thereby promoting operational agility and responsiveness to market demands.

Imagine a manufacturing environment where data regarding equipment performance, inventory status, and supply chain logistics is seamlessly transmitted in real time. Quantum-enhanced communication channels could enable machine learning algorithms to analyze data on-the-fly, optimizing production schedules and resource allocation dynamically. For instance, predictive maintenance powered by instantaneous data analysis can foresee equipment failures before they occur, minimizing downtime and reducing costs associated with emergency repairs. This evolution can lead to manufacturing environments that are not only more efficient but also more sustainable, as resources are deployed more judiciously based on real-time insights.

Moreover, the implications for quality control and assurance in manufacturing processes cannot be overstated. With Quantum Proxy facilitating real-time oversight, data related to product specifications, quality metrics, and customer feedback can flow freely between stakeholders. This immediate access to critical information enables organizations to make adjustments on the fly, ensuring that products meet quality standards and customer expectations without delay. The synergy between efficient production systems and guaranteed product quality consequently fosters stronger relationships between manufacturers and consumers, as trust in product reliability increases.

The broader shift towards interconnected, intelligent manufacturing systems—often termed Industry 4.0—will greatly benefit from the advancements made possible through quantum communication. As industries evolve toward greater automation, the ability to monitor processes and systems remotely while ensuring robust data security becomes vital. Quantum technologies enhance not only efficiency but also the integrity of the entire manufacturing ecosystem, aligning with industry-specific regulations and standards related to data protection.

Quantum Proxy can also usher in new paradigms when it comes to supply chain management. By providing end-to-end visibility across the entire supply chain—from suppliers to producers, to distributors —quantum-enhanced communication can facilitate better coordination among partners. Quantum networks could help track products in transit, allowing businesses to monitor environmental conditions and potential disruptions while providing immediate updates to all stakeholders. This high level of integration opens new avenues for optimization, efficiency, and risk mitigation, as organizations anticipate and adapt to fluctuations in demand and supply chain dynamics.

However, realizing the full potential of quantum technologies in manufacturing and industrial efficiency requires thoughtful consideration of the accompanying challenges. Significant investments in infrastructure will be necessary to implement these advanced systems, and the integration of quantum communication with existing technologies must be approached strategically. Furthermore, workforce training and education will be integral to equipping employees with the skills needed to navigate this quantum-driven landscape.

Additionally, as organizations embrace these tools, they must remain vigilant about the ethical implications that arise concerning data privacy, surveillance, and equitable access to quantum technologies. The commitment to fostering inclusive practices as quantum communication technologies evolve will ensure that the benefits do not disproportionately favor specific industries or demographics.

In conclusion, the integration of Quantum Proxy into manufacturing and industrial efficiency represents a transformative opportunity poised to redefine traditional production paradigms. By leveraging the capabilities of quantum communication technologies, industries can enhance operational efficiency, optimize resource management, and bolster product quality while maintaining relentless agility. As we embrace these advancements, our focus must remain anchored in ethical considerations, ensuring equitable access and responsible use of quantum technologies. The path ahead will not only heighten industrial capabilities but could usher in an era characterized by smarter manufacturing and interconnected systems that redefine the essence of efficiency in industrial practices.

10.5. Space Exploration and Quantum Navigation

Space exploration and the concept of quantum navigation represent a remarkable intersection of advanced science and human ambition. As humanity sets its sights on the cosmos, the application of quantum mechanics through technologies like Quantum Proxy opens exciting avenues for redefining how we approach space travel, navigation, and understanding the universe. In this subchapter, we will delve into the innovative concepts emerging from quantum mechanics and their potential to revolutionize space exploration.

The overarching theme of intertwining quantum principles with navigation lies in the concept of using entangled particles for precise measurement and real-time data transfer across expansive distances. In space exploration, where distances are vast and obstacles unpredictable, maintaining accurate orientation and communication becomes paramount. Traditional navigation systems rely on established frameworks—gyroscopes, GPS signals from satellites, and celestial navigation methods are all critical components, but they are susceptible to inaccuracies due to signal delays and environmental disruptions. Quantum navigation, empowered by the principles of entanglement and superposition, could enhance these systems significantly.

One compelling application of quantum navigation lies in utilizing entangled particles to create highly sensitive measurement devices known as quantum sensors. These sensors can detect minute fluctuations in gravitational fields, magnetic fields, and other spatial parameters critical for navigation. For example, quantum accelerometers could revolutionize how spacecraft and satellites determine their trajectory and position by measuring changes with unparalleled accuracy, even in environments devoid of external references. This capability could prove invaluable during deep-space missions, where traditional navigation aids may not be accessible.

Moreover, the integration of quantum communication technologies into space-based systems enhances real-time data sharing and communication between spacecraft and mission control on Earth. The ability to transmit quantum states has significant implications for the instantaneous communication of navigation data, ensuring that any corrections or adjustments made by navigational systems can be communicated without delay. Imagine a spacecraft exploring a distant planet, where the quantum communication system securely transmits navigational adjustments to ground control, allowing for immediate feedback and cooperative decision-making.

Additionally, the prospect of a Quantum Internet for space exploration is emerging as researchers visualize a network of quantum communicators operating on various celestial bodies. Quantum repeaters deployed on satellites or lunar facilities could facilitate long-distance data relay between space missions while maintaining the integrity and security of transmissions. This interconnectedness expands our capabilities to manage explorations efficiently, ensuring that each journey across the cosmos becomes an opportunity to deepen our understanding of both our immediate surroundings and the broader universe.

As we envision the future of quantum navigation in space exploration, it is crucial to consider the ramifications these advancements may have on scientific discovery. Quantum principles could enable precision mapping of celestial bodies and phenomena—planets, moons, comets, and asteroids—allowing researchers to analyze their geological compositions and dynamics with heightened accuracy. Furthermore, the ability to use quantum sensors to search for gravitational waves or other cosmic activities may yield insights into the fabric of space-time itself, challenging and expanding our understanding of fundamental physics.

However, the path toward integrating quantum navigation into space exploration is fraught with challenges that require meticulous consideration. The technology must undergo rigorous testing in various environments to ensure reliability and effectiveness. Additionally, addressing the potential for interference in space-based quantum systems necessitates collaborations across researchers and engineers to develop shielding and other protective measures that maintain quantum integrity.

Moreover, ethical considerations surrounding the deployment of these technologies in outer space should not be overlooked. As we expand our footprint beyond Earth, we must respect the integrity of celestial environments and consider the potential impact on existing ecosystems. The emergence of quantum navigation calls for international agreements and frameworks that govern the responsible exploration of space and the preservation of cosmic heritage.

In conclusion, the application of quantum navigation technologies in the realm of space exploration heralds an era where previously unimaginable possibilities come to fruition. The integration of quantum principles strengthens our navigation capabilities, enhances data transfer, and deepens our understanding of the universe. As we stand on the threshold of this quantum-driven future, the voyage into space awaits—where the advancements of Quantum Proxy pave the way for a new frontier of exploration, connection, and discovery beyond our world. The journey ahead invites us to embrace the convergence of quantum mechanics and space exploration, connecting us to the cosmos in ways that redefine human experience and understanding.

11. Envisioning the Future of Quantum Proxy

11.1. From Concept to Reality

In a world increasingly defined by technological advancements, the transition from conceptualizing Quantum Proxy to realizing it as a tangible technology represents a tantalizing frontier for scientists, engineers, and societies alike. The journey of Quantum Proxy—from theoretical foundations steeped in quantum mechanics to practical implementations that could redefine communication and presence—is one marked by ambition, collaboration, and the quest for innovative solutions.

As we embark on this passage from concept to reality, we must first recognize the fundamental principles underpinning Quantum Proxy, particularly quantum entanglement and superposition. These core attributes of quantum mechanics promise to enhance the way individuals connect and interact across distances, enabling instantaneous sharing of experiences that feel authentic and immediate. This shift could fundamentally alter human relationships, blurring the lines between physical co-presence and telecommunication in ways that have traditionally been confined to the realm of imagination.

To realize this vision, a diverse range of stakeholders must foster collaboration across disciplines. Researchers from academia, industry innovators, policymakers, and ethicists must work synergistically, engaging in dialogues that emphasize the nuances of quantum mechanics while accounting for the practical considerations that will shape the deployment of Quantum Proxy technologies. By facilitating constructive exchanges among these varied voices, we can grasp the complexities surrounding the integration of quantum communication systems in a manner that aligns with societal values.

The path to quantum ubiquity requires strategic investments in infrastructure and human capital to prepare for a future where quantum communication is seamlessly integrated into our daily lives. Governments and institutions must allocate resources for research and development projects focusing on quantum communication technologies, as well as education and training programs that equip individuals with the skills required to navigate this evolving landscape. Such commitment will ensure that society can adapt and thrive as advanced quantum solutions become accessible to a broader audience.

Moreover, the potential for Quantum Proxy to transform human experience and interaction cannot be overstated. As individuals harness its capabilities, we can envision immersive shared experiences, deepening emotional connections and improving collaboration in personal and professional realms. This transformation becomes particularly relevant in contexts such as remote work, education, and telemedicine, where the palpable sense of presence afforded by quantum communication can yield positive implications for engagement and outcomes.

Looking forward, a glimpse into future innovations reveals a panorama of possibilities facilitated by quantum advancements. We may envision educational landscapes that prioritize real-time interactions, enabling students from various backgrounds and locations to collaborate on projects seamlessly. Similarly, the entertainment industry could evolve to embrace participatory models, where audiences take a central role in shaping narratives through quantum-enabled interactions. These scenarios illustrate just a fraction of how Quantum Proxy could reframe everyday human experiences across sectors.

The global effects of integrating quantum communication technologies are likely to extend beyond the realms of individual interaction, promising shifts in cultural dynamics, economic systems, and professional landscapes. With the ability to connect individuals instantaneously, the potential for cultural exchange, knowledge transfer, and collaborative problem-solving expands exponentially, creating opportunities for global engagement that defy geographical constraints. These advances can foster a deeper appreciation of diverse perspectives, promoting empathy and understanding in an increasingly interconnected world.

As societies adapt to these transformative changes, it is imperative to remain mindful of the ethical considerations that accompany the deployment of Quantum Proxy. Normative frameworks must be developed to safeguard against potential overreach, ensuring that the benefits of quantum technologies enhance human dignity and authenticity rather than erode them. Continuous dialogue among stakeholders must prioritize individual rights, consent, and inclusive access to create a landscape where technology serves as a force for good.

In conclusion, the evolution from concept to reality for Quantum Proxy represents a remarkable journey embedded in ambition, innovation, and collaborative spirit. Embracing the foundational principles of quantum mechanics, fostering interdisciplinary partnerships, and prioritizing ethical considerations will ultimately shape the profound effects of quantum communication technologies on human experiences. As we strive for quantum ubiquity, we open the door to a world where presence redefines the constructs of communication, paving the way for an enriched future where connections are instant, authentic, and deeply resonant. The horizon ahead invites us to embrace the extraordinary potential of Quantum Proxy, ushering in a new era of human interaction that transcends distance and illuminates the path forward.

11.2. The Path to Quantum Ubiquity

In an era where technological advancements continuously redefine our existence, the path to quantum ubiquity emerges as a transformative journey marked by promise and potential. The advent of Quantum Proxy lays the groundwork for a future where communication and interaction transcend the limitations of distance, allowing individuals to engage authentically and meaningfully, regardless of their geographical locations.

The notion of quantum ubiquity rests on the fundamental principles of quantum mechanics, particularly the phenomena of entanglement and superposition. By harnessing these properties, Quantum Proxy offers a vision of seamless communication characterized by real-time connectivity and immersive experiences. As we explore this path, it becomes evident that the transition from theoretical concepts to practical applications hinges on innovative collaboration across disciplines, industries, and nations.

The journey toward quantum ubiquity necessitates active engagement from various stakeholders, including researchers, engineers, policymakers, and community members. Scientific collaboration embodies the essence of this endeavor, as institutions pool resources and expertise to advance quantum communication technologies. The establishment of international research consortia and partnerships exemplifies the unification of expertise necessary for tackling the complexities associated with integrating quantum principles into communication systems. By fostering diverse collaborations, we can pool knowledge and creativity to accelerate the realization of Quantum Proxy.

Transforming human experience and interaction through Quantum Proxy entails a fundamental reimagining of how we connect with one another. Picture a world where physical distance becomes insignificant, and individuals can share experiences and emotions in real-time as if they were co-located. This transformation holds profound implications for personal relationships, professional collaboration, and cultural exchanges. Quantum Proxy can redefine conventional notions of presence, allowing for deeper and more meaningful connections that resonate on emotional and experiential levels.

The vision of quantum ubiquity extends to various sectors, including education, healthcare, and entertainment. In educational contexts, students could engage with global experts and participate in collaborative learning experiences that challenge traditional classroom boundaries. Healthcare providers could conduct secure telemedicine consultations, sharing vital patient information without the limitations of conventional communication. The entertainment industry could facilitate immersive storytelling experiences where audience engagement becomes interactive and participatory, enhancing the richness of cultural expressions.

However, as we traverse the path to quantum ubiquity, ethical considerations must remain at the forefront of our advancement efforts. It is imperative to establish frameworks that safeguard individual rights, privacy, and inclusivity within the quantum landscape. The advantages of quantum communication should not be confined to privileged groups but should be accessible to all, enabling equitable participation in the interconnected future. Addressing concerns surrounding surveillance, consent, and data ownership is vital to navigating the ethical complexities that accompany the integration of Quantum Proxy.

The road ahead unfolds with a glimpse into future innovations. As researchers continue to refine and enhance quantum communication technologies, the potential to unlock new capabilities will lead to unexpected applications. From revolutionizing collaborative workflows to streamlining logistics and supply chains through real-time data transfer, the possibilities are vast. Future innovations in quantum systems could catalyze breakthroughs in artificial intelligence, personalized medicine, and climate modeling, ultimately reshaping our understanding of the universe and our place within it.

Furthermore, the global effects of adopting Quantum Proxy will extend to cultural dynamics and societal structures. By facilitating instantaneous interactions, the potential for cultural exchange will deepen, fostering empathy and understanding across diverse populations. The ripple effects of quantum-enhanced communication may transform how we perceive connections within our communities and beyond, reinforcing the interconnectedness of humanity in a rapidly evolving world.

As we embark on this journey toward quantum ubiquity, it is important to adapt and remain responsive to the challenges and opportunities that arise. The path to realizing the potential of Quantum Proxy necessitates a commitment to interdisciplinary cooperation, ethical stewardship, and inclusive practices. By harnessing the power of quantum mechanics and nurturing the collaborative spirit that fuels this progress, we can uncover new paradigms for communication and connection that resonate with authenticity and shared human experience.

In conclusion, the path to quantum ubiquity indicates a future where Quantum Proxy transforms the essence of communication, reshaping our interactions and relationships across the globe. By witnessing the convergence of technology with human experience, we stand poised to redefine presence itself, embarking on a remarkable journey toward enriched connections, profound understanding, and an inter-connected existence that transcends the limitations of distance. The quantum revolution beckons us forward, offering opportunities to reimagine our world and redefine what it means to truly connect with one another in the age of telepresence.

11.3. Transforming Human Experience and Interaction

The exploration of transforming human experience and interaction through Quantum Proxy presents a captivating narrative filled with profound implications for the way individuals connect, communicate, and relate to one another in an increasingly digital world. As the technology behind Quantum Proxy evolves, driven by the principles of quantum mechanics, we find ourselves on the brink of what could be termed a new epoch in human connectivity—one that transcends traditional boundaries and redefines presence itself.

At the heart of this transformative capability lies quantum entangle-ment, which enables the instantaneous sharing of information across vast distances. This unique aspect of quantum communication fun-damentally alters the traditional notions of communication, where delays and barriers typically impede genuine interaction. By elimi-nating these constraints, Quantum Proxy allows people to engage with each other as if they were physically together, creating authentic connections that resonate on emotional levels. Imagine the possibil-ities of sharing life's important moments—celebrations, milestones, or even everyday interactions—in real-time, feeling the vibrancy of connection despite the physical distances that may separate us.

The benefits of such a transformation extend well beyond mere enhancements to remote communication. Industries such as education, healthcare, and entertainment are ripe for disruption, with quantum-enhanced experiences ushering in new paradigms of engagement. In educational settings, students from diverse backgrounds could collaboratively tackle projects, access lectures from leading experts globally, and bond over immersive learning experiences that enrich their understanding of complex subjects. Healthcare professionals may utilize quantum communication to conduct secure telemedicine consultations, allowing for immediate and nuanced interactions that improve patient care outcomes. Meanwhile, the entertainment industry could evolve to accommodate interactive storytelling frameworks, where audiences actively shape narratives, fostering deeper emotional ties to the content being consumed.

As we envision a future where Quantum Proxy technologies become integrated into everyday life, it's important to address the corresponding shifts in social dynamics and ethical considerations. The transformation of human experience facilitated by quantum communication raises questions surrounding privacy, data ownership, and equity. In a world defined by enhanced connectivity, ensuring that these technologies are accessible to all and do not exacerbate existing social inequalities becomes a paramount concern. Moreover, it will be essential to navigate the ethical ramifications of immersive shared experiences, particularly surrounding consent and the potential for surveillance in increasingly interconnected environments.

In examining the tangible impacts of these developments, we must also grapple with the implications for culture and community. The ability to connect authentically and in real-time fosters an enhanced sense of belonging and shared experience. Audiences that engage with one another around global events, performances, or significant life moments cultivate a tapestry of interconnectedness that transcends geography. This interwoven narrative creates a rich cultural landscape where diverse voices, ideas, and customs interact and enrich one another, ultimately fostering mutual understanding and empathy in a world that often feels divided.

A glimpse into future innovations unveils a spectrum of possibilities that Quantum Proxy could unlock for human interaction. As research initiatives advance, we may witness the emergence of virtual reality environments built on quantum technologies that provide even more immersive experiences. Such innovations could change how we perceive and interact within our environments, with further developments in haptic feedback enabling a wider range of sensory engagement in virtual spaces.

In summary, transforming human experience and interaction through Quantum Proxy presents a compelling vision for a future characterized by authentic connections that transcend traditional barriers. As we explore the implications of this technological transformation, it becomes increasingly vital to remain attuned to the ethical and societal considerations that accompany these advancements. The ability to engage with one another instantaneously through quantum communication enriches our lives in profound ways, propelling us to reimagine the very fabric of human relationships and the essence of presence itself in an interconnected world. As we chart our future and navigate the complexities introduced by Quantum Proxy, we lay the foundations for a more connected and empathetic global society, where the potential for transformation is as boundless as the universe itself.

11.4. A Glimpse into Future Innovations

In the rapidly evolving landscape of technology, particularly within the realm of quantum communication and the promise of Quantum Proxy, we find ourselves on the threshold of several innovations that could profoundly reshape human experience and interaction. These innovations promise to transcend the limitations of traditional communication methods and redefine the very nature of connectivity, presence, and collaboration across various sectors.

One significant area for future exploration lies in the development of sophisticated quantum communication networks. As researchers lay the groundwork for a Quantum Internet, a new era of instantaneous data sharing may emerge, characterized by its inherent security and efficiency. Unlike classical systems, where signal degradation and latency can hinder communication, quantum communication could offer seamless interactions among users across vast distances, allowing for real-time collaboration and engagement. The implications for education are substantial; classrooms could connect globally, enabling students to engage with experts and peers from different cultures and backgrounds, cultivating an enriched learning experience that transcends geographical boundaries.

Moreover, the integration of quantum technologies into virtual and augmented reality environments could revolutionize how we perceive and interact with digital content. Imagine immersive simulations where individuals can collaboratively explore spaces, participate in experiments, or engage in experiential learning, all while feeling a genuine sense of presence. Quantum Proxy could enable shared experiences that enhance emotional engagement, allowing users to interact meaningfully as if they were co-located. Such innovations would be monumental in sectors such as training and development, where hands-on experience is crucial for skill acquisition.

In the healthcare realm, the potential for Quantum Proxy technologies to transform telemedicine cannot be overstated. As quantum communication systems facilitate immediate and secure exchanges of medical information, healthcare providers could conduct consultations that feel as intimate and personal as in-office visits. Imagine a scenario where a doctor can monitor a patient's vital signs or examine test results in real-time through a quantum-enabled platform, leading to timely interventions and improved patient outcomes. This shift holds the promise of making healthcare more accessible and personalized, ultimately bridging the gaps that have long existed due to distance.

The entertainment industry also stands to benefit significantly from quantum innovations. As Quantum Proxy technologies enable immersive and interactive storytelling experiences, audiences could become active participants in narratives, shaping the direction of a film or game collaboratively. This participatory model enriches the viewer's connection to the content and could lead to entirely new genres and modes of consumption that push the boundaries of storytelling. Furthermore, live events such as concerts, performances, and exhibitions could transform into collective experiences that draw audiences together from all corners of the globe, fostering a sense of community and shared culture.

Despite the promise of these future innovations, several questions remain unanswered. As quantum communication technologies develop, how can we ensure that access is equitable and that marginalized communities do not fall behind? In the rush to adopt new technologies, it is vital to create frameworks that protect individual rights, ensure privacy, and address ethical concerns surrounding data security and surveillance. The responsibility to navigate these challenges must be shared among researchers, policymakers, and industry leaders, who must prioritize ethical considerations as they innovate.

Moreover, as Quantum Proxy redefines communication norms, how will our understanding of relationships and social dynamics evolve? With instant and immersive interactions becoming commonplace, there may be shifts in how we perceive physical presence, intimacy, and authenticity in our connections. Balancing the technological benefits with the emotional and cultural implications of these changes will be crucial in fostering interactions that are enriching rather than superficial.

As we envision these future innovations, the overarching takeaway is the importance of collaboration across disciplines and borders. The advancement of Quantum Proxy necessitates the integration of knowledge and expertise from diverse fields, paving the way for pioneering solutions that maximize the technology's potential. By working together in a spirit of cooperation and inclusiveness, we can harness the transformative power of quantum technologies to foster a more connected, empathetic, and innovative society.

In conclusion, the path to realizing the full potential of Quantum Proxy promises an exciting future filled with innovations that redefine communication, presence, and the very nature of human interaction. As we consider the endless possibilities that lie ahead, we must also remain vigilant about the ethical and societal implications of these advancements. The commitment to responsible innovation, equitable access, and inclusive practices will ultimately shape a world where quantum technologies serve to enrich our lives, connect us more deeply, and empower us to navigate the complexities of an interconnected existence. The journey forward will be one of discovery, collaboration, and transformation, as we embrace the capabilities of quantum mechanics to redefine the human experience.

11.5. Global Effects and Adaptation

The global effects of technological advancements, particularly those stemming from Quantum Proxy, are poised to instigate profound changes across various facets of society. As the principles of quantum mechanics permeate communication through entangled particles and instantaneous data sharing, nations, communities, and individuals will need to adapt to a new paradigm of interaction. The following exploration encapsulates how these transformative effects might unfold, necessitating adaptation at multiple levels—from individual behaviors to institutional practices and international frameworks.

At the heart of these changes lies the enhancement of communication capabilities, which alters the dynamics of personal relationships and social interactions. Quantum Proxy holds the potential to revolutionize how individuals connect across distances, facilitating real-time interactions that carry the emotional and sensory depth of physical presence. This shift could redefine global dynamics, enabling families and friends separated by geographical barriers to engage authentically, thus strengthening interpersonal bonds. As people become accustomed to these rich telepresence experiences, traditional forms of communication may be perceived as insufficient, compelling a cultural shift towards embracing advanced technologies in daily interactions.

In professional contexts, the implications are equally significant. Industries across the globe will need to adapt their workflows and collaboration practices to leverage the offerings of quantum-enhanced communication. Business meetings, strategy sessions, and project collaborations may shift from periodic face-to-face encounters to ongoing real-time engagements that feel more connected and immediate. Organizations will need to invest in the infrastructure that supports these advancements, including quantum networks and collaborative platforms optimized for quantum interactions. As companies evolve to integrate these technologies, existing paradigms in workforce dynamics may be disrupted, requiring new considerations around training, leadership, and organizational culture.

Beyond interpersonal and professional spheres, the broader societal implications of quantum communication will demand systemic adaptations. Governments and policymakers will need to address the ethical and legal challenges posed by the deployment of quantum technologies. Issues surrounding data privacy, consent, and security will emerge as critical focal points as society grapples with the technology's capability to facilitate real-time monitoring and potential surveillance. Crafting regulatory frameworks that ensure responsible use and protect individual rights in the context of quantum-enhanced communication will be paramount to ensuring that these technologies are embraced rather than feared by the public.

Moreover, adapting to the shifts brought about by Quantum Proxy requires a reconsideration of educational paradigms. As quantum technologies infiltrate classrooms, the traditional modes of knowledge transfer and engagement will evolve. Students will need to acquire skills and competencies that enable them to thrive in an increasingly interconnected, technologically sophisticated world. Educational institutions will need to embrace interdisciplinary approaches that foster a deep understanding of both quantum principles and ethical considerations surrounding their application.

The economic landscape will also experience ramifications as Quantum Proxy leads to new models of service delivery and communication. Sectors such as healthcare can expect significant advancements in telemedicine that enhance patient experiences, improve outcomes, and streamline care processes. The potential for real-time access to specialized knowledge and expertise could democratize healthcare access, ensuring that underserved communities benefit from advancements in medical technology. To fully realize these benefits, systems must be put in place to ensure equitable access across populations, addressing gaps created by socio-economic divides.

While the promise of quantum technologies is vast, it is essential to remain mindful of the disparities that may arise in global contexts. As nations adopt quantum communication systems at different paces, there exists a risk that advanced capabilities may privilege some countries over others, reinforcing existing power imbalances. It is crucial for international collaborations and efforts to promote knowledge transfer and technology sharing, allowing broader access to the advantages offered by quantum technologies so that no community is left behind.

In conclusion, the global effects and adaptations necessitated by Quantum Proxy and its underlying quantum principles represent a multifaceted transformation that stretches across the unique dimensions of human experience, societal structures, and institutional frameworks. Embracing this evolution demands proactive efforts from individuals, organizations, and governments to navigate the opportunities and challenges introduced by quantum advancements. Through conscious adaptation, we can harness the full potential of Quantum Proxy to enrich connections, foster equitable access, and redefine communication on a global scale, creating a future where distance is trivialized, and human relationships can thrive in the quantum realm.

www.ingramcontent.com/pod-product-compliance
Lightning Source LLC
LaVergne TN
LVHW051653050326
832903LV00032B/3777